TIE ON YOUR APRON in the KITCHEN of PRAYER

BECKY REESER TERRY

Taste and see that the Lord is good!
Psalm 34:8

Tie on your Apron in the Kitchen of Prayer

Copyright © 2021 by Becky Reeser Terry

All rights reserved

Cover and interior design by Roseanna M. White

Unless otherwise indicated, Scripture quotations are taken from the Holy Bible, New International Version, NIV Copyright © 1973, 1978, 1984, 2011 by Biblica, Inc. Used by permission. All rights reserved worldwide.

Scriptures marked NASB are taken from the New American Standard Bible, © 1960, 1971, 1973 by The Lockman Foundation. Used by permission. All rights reserved.

www.lockman.org

Regarding the resources given under Pantry Provisions, permission has been generously granted by the author, Sylvia Gunter, and her ministry, The Father's Business.

ISBN: 978-0-578-98431-5 (spiral bound)
978-0-578-37883-1 (paperback)

To my immediate family ~
Jim
Meg
Sara Beth
Dexter
Griffin
...and all those to come.
You have my heart; you are my home.

To my extended family ~
You have made my life a feast.

To my friends ~
All the world's five-star meals cannot compare.

To my God ~
Thank You for inviting me to Your banquet table!

In loving memory of ~
My dear Babs
Miss your brownies; miss *you* more.

My beloved mom
Miss your macaroni and cheese; miss *you* more.

My treasured grandmom
Miss your chicken noodle soup; miss *you* more.

From my kitchen to yours, welcome!

Like many of you, I am well-acquainted with the kitchen—maybe more than most. My mother's side of the family owned and ran a family restaurant for over fifty years, and that diner became my second home. I did everything from peeling buckets of potatoes and making salads, to washing dishes and busing tables. I was hostess, cashier, and waitress—sometimes all three at once!

Called the Limerick Diner, because of its location in Limerick, Pennsylvania, this popular hangout kept its doors open 24/7. The original diner was the typical stainless-steel exterior in the shape of an Airstream trailer. The interior accommodated two sets of counters with stools and booths running the length of the building. The iconic jukeboxes at each booth played the personally selected hit tunes of the day. People came from near and far to enjoy the delicious homemade food, with the famous Chicken Pot Pie and Rice Pudding topping the list of favorites.

Over time the diner became a bigger, more modern restaurant, built to accommodate the multitudes of guests. It eventually could seat 265 people, but we often ended up with a line of waiting customers during peak hours. For many years the diner landed on the list of the top 200 of independent restaurants in the USA, according to the industry magazine, *Restaurant News*.

Gleaming stainless steel ruled the cavernous kitchen from the dishwasher to the salad station, and from the steam table to the fryolaters. Multiple ovens and stove burners put out constant heat, producing stifling temps during the summer months. Then I wouldn't mind a prankster "locking" me in the massive walk-in freezer by holding the door shut on me for a minute or so!

The "back room," where all the prep work was done, hummed with three to four men and women going about their work, while chatting about their lives or the latest TV show viewed the night before. "Potato Charlie," king of his castle in the potato room, sat on an overturned white bucket and peeled and eyed hundreds of potatoes before cutting them into french fries.

When employees entered the back door, they clocked in, and the waitresses checked the schedule taped on the wall to see their assigned stations for their day or night shift. The symbiotic dance between the waitresses and "the hub," the spinning silver wheel where they attached the customers' orders, and the kitchen staff as they called out and prepared the orders, always came under fire for accuracy and speed. In true diner fashion, an impatient "Pick up!" launched from the kitchen could be heard out front, if an order wasn't delivered promptly to the customer.

My grandmother, "Mother Moore," as she was lovingly called, was the iconic fixture of the diner. A diminutive dynamo, she worked as a cook in her son and daughter-in-law's restaurant six days a week, until she was in her eighties. Customers and employees revered and respected her for her food and for her grace and age. I rarely saw her without her white butcher apron, which she always gussied up with a brooch of some sort. I still recall the crescent moon pin with a cloverleaf in the middle.

At a small table for two, away from the hustle-bustle, my aunt typed the day's menu, listing the entree specials, vegetables, and desserts, which changed daily. At night my grandmother sat there with a large stainless-steel bowl cutting up vegetables for soups. My grandmother's hands always smelled like onions, and to this day I love the smell of onions on my hands.

The daily schedule included changing out the cash register drawer at 8:00 a.m., 4:00 p.m., and 12:00 a.m. Typically, my uncle would handle the exchange in the morning, my aunt in the afternoon, and my grandmother at midnight. Looking back, I shake my head in wonder and thanksgiving that my little old grandmother, who stood under five feet tall, was not robbed.

Those years working in the diner fostered many fond memories for me.

We had lots of "regulars," mostly men who stopped in every day for at least one of their meals and sometimes all three. One such man was Otto, a shy guy with dark hair and glasses, who would come in every evening for dinner and sit at the counter. He always wore buttoned plaid shirts with dress pants, and Aunt Ruthie would "wait" on him. One night when he ordered a favorite dessert that was sold out, my aunt asked if he would like to come to her house—handily within walking distance—for a piece of homemade cake. They soon married, ending his nightly dinners at the diner, and they enjoyed a lovely life together until his passing.

One of my favorite memories belongs to an unforgettable breakfast order from a man with very specific instructions. He told me, "Eggs over easy. Not too greasy. Flip 'em and flop 'em, but don't drop 'em."

I walked a lot of steps over the years at the diner and saw a multitude of people come and go. The people that came through the doors of the diner had one thing in common—hunger. But it wasn't just physical hunger. They were hungry souls looking for connection. Couples talked about their relationships, business associates worked on coming to a "meeting of the minds," and birthdays and anniversaries were celebrated. A grandmother brought her grandson for a special pancake breakfast, and lonely sojourners sought a smile and small talk. I saw a lot of unspoken hurt and pain in hunched shoulders, piercing eyes, and the occasional rudeness.

Spirits were hungry too. I interacted with all ages and stages of life on a daily basis, from babies to the elderly. Some I saw only once and some I saw daily for years. Oh, to think now, how Jesus loved them! How I wish they could have known that! How amazingly blessed I am that I found that to be true—in a kitchen.

I remember vividly, over four decades now, sitting on the

counter in our apartment's tiny kitchen as my roommate, Beverly, explained to me who Jesus is—fully God and fully man. She told me how He left the glory of heaven to die on the Cross for the forgiveness of my sins so that I could be reconciled to my holy Father God. One week shy of my 21st birthday, I made the greatest decision of my life! I realized how prayer played a major role in my coming to know Jesus as my Savior and Lord, when I learned that Beverly's workplace Bible study group had been praying for me.

The kitchen, lovingly referred to as the "heart of the home," physically sustains us as the place where we store, prepare, and eat our food while connecting with family members. Now that my children are grown, the kitchen where I spend most of my time is my "prayer kitchen." Prayer, then, is the "heart of our spiritual home." It nourishes us spiritually in our minds, souls, and spirits as we connect with our heavenly family: the Holy Spirit who interprets our prayers for us, Jesus who intercedes for us, and Father God who answers our prayers.

Spending time in the kitchen of prayer melds together heaven and earth like your favorite food combination. Is yours peanut butter and jelly, biscuits and gravy, or pie and ice cream? Each one is a perfectly delicious pairing!

While many tell of a life-changing event or a dramatic prayer experience to recount their prayer journeys, that isn't my story. My motivation in prayer is simple: If Jesus, the Son of God, made prayer a priority because of its importance, how much more should I? I love Jesus, and I want to live a life that's pleasing to Him. I long to follow Him, honor Him, and give

Him glory for His Kingdom. I view prayer as the catalyst to fulfill those desires.

Scripture makes it very clear as to the significance and power of prayer. Why would I not want to make it a priority? I may be a suburban homemaker, but prayer allows me to go to Judea and Samaria and to all the ends of the earth. Prayer places me in a hospital room or in a college dorm. Most important, by prayer I enter God's Throne Room with confidence, where all grace, mercy, and power dwell. It turns an ordinary day *in* God's Kingdom into an extraordinary day *for* God's Kingdom.

Jesus is the reason we live, move, and have our being (Acts 17:28). Jesus is the reason we are blessed abundantly (John 10:10). Don't you want to be in communication with that Person? God tells us in Jeremiah 33:3, "Call to me and I will answer you and tell you great and unsearchable things you do not know." Don't you want to know what He wants to tell you?

God in His love and faithfulness has called us into fellowship with His Son, Jesus Christ our Lord (1 Corinthians 1:9). Are you fellowshipping with Him?

British writer C.S. Lewis describes it this way: "God designed the human machine to run on Himself. He Himself is the fuel our spirits were designed to burn, or the food our spirits were designed to feed on. There is no other." Without prayer we are refusing the food and ignoring the fellowship that gives us abundant life.

I wrote this study with you in mind, a woman who desires to be fed by Jesus. There's no right or wrong way to do this study. You can set your own pace and do as little or as much as you like in one sitting. You may choose to do it with one or two friends or in a Bible study setting with several.

Whether you choose to partake of a morsel or a meal when you come to your "kitchen of prayer," I hope and pray each bite will bring you nourishment and sustenance. And I pray by the end of our dining together that you'll know and love our faithful God in a more intimate way than ever before—and will want to continue a running conversation with Him.

THE FEAST OF PRAYER

For the most part, our lives are fast paced. Our minds and bodies are continually otherwise occupied, which leaves little room for talking to God. As pastor and author Samuel Chadwick (1860-1932) said, "Hurry is the death of prayer." May I ask, is the busyness and hustle of life really accomplishing what you want and need to get done? Oswald Chambers (1874-1917) says it succinctly and truthfully: "Prayer does not fit us for the greater work; prayer is the greater work." Let's take that wise advice from our spiritual forefathers and remember to slow down...not just today, but every day, reminding ourselves of the importance of prayer—and actually doing it.

Let's first explore the inexhaustible magnitude of prayer.

JESUS MODELED THE SIGNIFICANCE OF PRAYER

Write: Matthew 14:23

Write: Mark 1:35

Write: Luke 5:16

Write: Luke 6:12

Jesus, our All-in-All, is our Master and Mentor for our prayer life.

To whom did Jesus pray?

Where did Jesus pray?

When did Jesus pray?

With whom did Jesus pray?

Write and/or sketch observations you see in Jesus's prayer life. Talk to Jesus about ways that His example can spur you on in your prayer life.

Here are some hacks to up your prayer time from empty calorie snacking to nutritious gourmet feasting:

- ❖ Turn off the radio in the car
- ❖ Turn off the podcast on your jog
- ❖ Guard your Quiet Time fiercely (no appointments/commitments unless necessary)
- ❖ Turn off the TV for one show
- ❖ Limit social media scrolling to an appointed time per day (set your timer on your phone)
- ❖ Keep your phone across the room on silent mode
- ❖ Keep a pad and pen close by to jot down distractions that derail your focus

Be intentional about solitude.

> Without solitude, it is virtually impossible to live a spiritual life. We do not take the spiritual life seriously if we do not set aside time to be with God and listen to Him.
> – Henri Nouwen

Be still and know that I am God (Psalm 46:10).

ᏢRAYER IS AN ACT OF OBEDIENCE

God's Word calls us to pray. Take notes as you look up the following scriptures. Then write a synopsis and talk to God about it.

Romans 12:12

Ephesians 6:18

Philippians 4:4-8

Colossians 4:2

1 Thessalonians 5:17

PRAYER IS SPIRITUAL WARFARE

Make no mistake about it, we are engaged in a war against an enemy.

For our struggle is not against flesh and blood, but against the rulers, against the authorities, against the powers of this dark world and against the spiritual forces of evil in the heavenly realms (Ephesians 6:12).

Be alert and of sober mind. Your enemy, the devil, prowls around like a roaring lion looking for someone to devour (1 Peter 5:8).

Your prayers of faith glue shut, with Christ's victorious blood, the roaring lion's mouth that seeks to devour, and Satan cannot even get a nibble.

Darlene Deibler Rose served as a missionary in Papua New Guinea. When World War II broke out, she was sent to a Japanese prison camp where she endured four years of captivity. In her autobiography, *Evidence Not Seen: A Woman's Miraculous Faith in a Japanese Prison Camp of World War II*, Darlene speaks of unimaginable conditions, cruel treatment, an unthinkable diet, and near-death experiences. Prayer remained her constant sustenance.

She tells of one of her brushes with death. (The following incident took place before she was sent to a prison camp while still in grave danger. Her husband had already been sent to a prison camp and did not survive.) In the hallway of her home, she came face to face with a bandit carrying a machete in striking position. Although a self-described coward, she charged, and the bandit fled. "We heard bandits return several nights after that, but they never entered the house. It wasn't until after the war that I learned why. I had suspected the Jaffrey's gardener; he was Boegis, and he knew the layout of the house. When I asked him why they never entered the house again, he answered incredulously, 'Because of those people you had there – those people in white who stood about the house.' The Lord had put His angels around us. He had delivered."

PRAYER RELEASES GOD'S POWER AND LOVE

READ: LUKE 3:21-22

What was Jesus doing as He was being baptized?

What happened? Heaven opened!

> "Heaven is filled with the life and power and blessing earth needs, and the prayer of earth is the power to bring it down."
> –Andrew Murray (1828-1917)

PRAYER IS AN ACT OF SERVICE

Mysteriously, we are participating in God's work. He has established prayer as part of His plan for accomplishing His will on earth. We may not be able to serve others and build God's Kingdom physically or financially as our hearts desire, but our prayers do.

Before they call I will answer; while they are still speaking I will hear (Isaiah 65:24).

Holocaust survivor Corrie ten Boom stated, "The wonderful thing about praying is that you leave a world of not being able to do something and enter God's realm where everything is possible."

Write: Luke 1:37

Write: Hebrews 4:16

PRAYER IS A FORM OF SELF-CARE

Casting all your anxiety on Him because He cares for you (1 Peter 5:7) is a therapeutic stress reliever. Prayer brings the peace God gave us and wants us to have. Don't we want that peace? Pray. I used to be bad about going to the telephone and calling a girlfriend about my problems. Now I go to the One who can fix it and bring me peace. Much better!

Talking things out with the One who knows all and holds all wisdom gives us clarity and a better understanding of ourselves, others, and the world around us. It drains the negative of its power while it increases our faith. It brings into sharper focus who God is, who we are in Christ, and reminds us of His promises. It washes away lies, feelings, and circumstances that we weren't meant to carry and cleanses us with Truth—a spiritual, warm bath.

PRAYER DEEPENS OUR RELATIONSHIP WITH GOD

It is important to remember that prayer is about our relationship with God—the most important relationship we have. "Self" is relentless in wanting to be the most important relationship we have. It constantly pursues us to live a life of all things "self": self-centeredness, self-controlling, self-absorbed, self-righteous, self-pitying. Self is masterful at distancing us from God, which is just the opposite of what God wants.

Prayer is the remedy. It is the instant connection that breaks through the barrier of self and brings us back to what our center is—our relationship with God. The more we pray, the stronger our bond with Him. The stronger our bond with Him, the more we become like Him. The more we become like Him, the more glory we can bring to Him. The highest purpose of prayer is to bring Him glory.

> "Prayer, per se, is not the object—God is. Prayer doesn't work. God works in answer to prayer. Remember that He does not give answers. He is the Answer. It is more important who He is than what He does for you. God does not share His glory with those who come to use Him."
> —Sylvia Gunter

Write: John 14:13

Read: John 15:5-8

What does God want us to do? (vs. 7)

What will be the result and why? (vss. 7-8)

Keep in mind that I wrote this Bible study to encourage, not to induce guilt. Trust me, I'm not "there" yet in my prayer life. None of us ever will be. I've read several quotes from those we consider "spiritual giants of the faith" who speak of their prayer lives not being what they wished. So please be only encouraged, dear one.

YOUR BOUNTIFUL SPIRITUAL KITCHEN

Our spiritual kitchens are amazing!

The place we pray is the Throne Room where we can approach God with freedom and confidence (see Eph. 3:12).

We have the greatest executive chef with an infinite number of Michelin stars—the Bread of Life Himself. His divine power has bestowed on us everything pertaining to life and godliness, through the true knowledge of Him who called us by His own glory and power (see 2 Peter 1:3 NASB). No matter what your needs, God is and God provides.

God has given us a "pantry" that is fully stocked beyond our imaginations. We can walk into it and find exactly what we need at all times. It miraculously never gets depleted or disarrayed, dusty and out-of-reach like the aged Crock-Pot you can't get rid of just in case you may need it. Everything in God's pantry is important and has a purpose. This pantry is the Word of God.

Praying God's Word is a critical component in our prayer lives. We see this in John 15:7-8, when Jesus told His disciples, "If you abide in me, and my words abide in you, ask whatever you wish, and it will be done for you. By this my Father is glorified, that you bear much fruit and so prove to be my disciples."

I have read that there are anywhere from 3,000 to 33,000 promises in the Bible. Enjoy 2 Corinthians 1:20: For no matter how many promises God has made, they are "Yes" in Christ. And so through Him the "Amen" is spoken by us to the glory of God.

Pray the promises. Press into Jesus and His "Yes." Declare the "Amen" to the glory of God.

We also see the magnitude of God's Word in Matthew 4:3-4, when Jesus used scripture while rebuking Satan: The tempter came to Him and said, "If You are the Son of God, tell these stones to become bread." Jesus answered, "It is written: 'Man shall not live on bread alone, but on every word that comes from the mouth of God.'"

The Word holds the power, the wisdom, and the victory.

TAKE NOTES ABOUT GOD'S WORD AS YOU LOOK UP THESE SCRIPTURES:

John 1:1

John 6:35

Psalm 119:103

Psalm 119:105

Jeremiah 15:16

Job 23:12

Now, put into your own words the importance of the Bread of Life and His Word in your prayers.

With the perfect kitchen, chef, and pantry, we don't have to worry about feeling inadequate as we cook in the kitchen of prayer. Jesus and the Holy Spirit do the "heavy lifting." Therefore, we do not have to be concerned about our ability or the efficacy of our prayers. The Holy Spirit takes our prayers, whether audible, groans, or tears of liquid intercession, and interprets them perfectly. Jesus then intercedes perfectly to Father God. Always. Our omniscient, omnipresent, and omnipotent God is not only hearing us, but also listening intently, caring about what we are saying, and relaying all our thoughts to the Throne Room, the perfect spiritual kitchen.

READ: ROMANS 8:26-39

Write in your own words and/or sketch what the Holy Spirit and Jesus are doing with our prayers and His love for us.

Take a moment to thank God for His immeasurable love, for the privilege and power of prayer, and for how Jesus and the Holy Spirit receive your prayers and intercede for you... perfectly!

It is our job to be the best sous-chefs we can be. In a professional kitchen, the sous-chef is the second in command. Sous in French means "under," which is fitting for our analogy since we place ourselves under the leadership and guidance of the Lord. In order for the executive chef to do His job, we as the sous-chefs must do ours first. Just as sous-chefs use their pantries copious times a day, we should use our spiritual pantry many times a day as well. Let's get cooking!

YOUR EARTHLY KITCHEN OF PRAYER

Imagine the kitchen of your dreams. Think of it as that favorite spot you'd call your "happy place." Would it be small and cozy but functional, with everything within reach? Utilitarian and professional—stainless steel surfaces and white tile, with cutting-edge appliances and clutter-free counters? Large, open, and light-filled? Homey and comfy, with kids' artwork and family photos? Or maybe it's your current kitchen or one that is familiar to you, like your grandmother's or a friend's? Perhaps the location is most important to you, whether it is tucked in the woods, or on a farm, or in a cottage on the beach.

Dream a little and describe or sketch it here.

Now put yourself in the welcoming kitchen of your imagination. A storm growls outside, but you feel safe and sheltered from the harsh elements. The aroma of your favorite comfort food wafts from the oven, providing a soothing balm to your weary soul. A knock on the door beckons as you hear your name lovingly called. When you fling open the door, Jesus is standing there.

Yes, Jesus desires to dine with you. He longs to spend time with you, listening as you share your heart with Him—your hopes, your dreams, your fears, your frustrations, your failures, your joy, your gratitude, and your needs.

You invite Him in, and as you peer into the face of your dinner companion, His pleasure electrifies your spirit with unexplainable love. The room is filled with peace, joy, and hope. The kitchen smells heavenly, the meal tastes divine, and the dinner guest is flawless. That is prayer, my friend.

We see throughout the Gospels that Jesus loved dining. Yet it wasn't the food He craved, but the communing, the conversation, the close connection. And so it is with you and me. The Lover of your soul, the One who knows you best and delights in you most, wants to daily commune, converse, and connect with you in an intimate way.

One of my favorite titles of Jesus, and the beautiful imagery it evokes, is the Good Shepherd. And hallelujah, we are the sheep of His pasture. Shepherds in biblical times had to stay with their sheep. They dined together. Jesus wants us to dine together. He wants us to know Him and to recognize His voice.

READ: PSALM 23

Reread it. Read it again. It is so rich with our Lord's attributes and kindness toward us.

Write a note to the Good Shepherd about all the things you see in this psalm regarding who God is and what He does for you. Or you can draw those things. Either way, be sure to give Him praise and thanks!

TIE ON YOUR APRON OF PRAYER

I love aprons. I collect vintage aprons. Although I have many, I have a hard time passing them up at an antique store. My favorite vintage aprons are waist aprons made with gingham fabric and embellished with a cross-stitch design, rickrack, and huge pockets. These were popular in the '50s and '60s, the era of my childhood. Then aprons were in vogue as a symbol of family and the comforts of home, so desperately needed after the ravages of World War II, which tore families apart.

Magazine ads often depicted women wearing these little domestic dresses. Girls in high school sewed them in home economics class as a common rite of passage. I particularly love the pockets because they connected with the hands of the women wearing them. The pockets carried the hankies that wiped tears, the clothespins that hung laundry, and the safety pins that came in handy in a pinch. Pockets held the peppermint to treat a child, the grocery list for the next visit to the store, and even prayers written and tucked away to be close to the wearer.

I even found on Amazon a little prayer book that could fit conveniently in an apron pocket, titled *The Apron-Pocket Book of Meditation and Prayer*, published in 1958. It must have been popular, since mine says it is the Sixth Printing. I also discovered *The Second Apron-Pocket Book of Meditation and Prayer*, published in 1963. I love envisioning godly women taking a moment or two out of their busy days to pray.

I think I love aprons the most because the women dearest to me wore them for much of their lives, especially one of my heroes, my mom. I now own her turquoise gingham apron. A tireless worker, my mom would come home from her job and not sit down until she fixed her family dinner and washed the dishes. (She was particular and didn't want us kids to help.) She always kept our house neat and clean, doing exceptionally thorough cleanings from top to bottom before Christmas and in the spring. When new linoleum was needed in the kitchen, my mother installed it herself.

Aprons represent love and service. Prayer, too, represents love and service.

READ: JOHN 13:1-17

Jesus wore an "apron," a makeshift apron when He wrapped a towel around His waist. (vs. 4)

How did Jesus love His disciples? (vs. 1)

How did He serve them? (vs. 5)

Why did He serve them? (vss. 12-16)

What is the result of our obedience when we serve one another? (vs. 17)

In our culture we don't make a practice of washing one another's feet. Yet Jesus's powerful example of humility and service is a beautiful reminder that we can all be of service in God's Kingdom, and prayer is a monumental way to serve others. Not only do we bless others, but we are blessed as well.

My waitress apron at the diner had two big pockets. One side carried my green-lined "Guest Check" order pad and pen, to note what I was going to serve the guests. The other side held my "tip" money—all coins and bills back then—what I was given in return for the service. It is through serving that we often receive blessings.

Emilie Griffin in her book, *Clinging: The Experience of Prayer*, suggests the goal in prayer is to give oneself away. We give ourselves away in prayer by offering our time, our attention, and our hearts.

At the wedding in Cana, the wine had run out, and Jesus had the servants pour water into large jars. The servants obeyed and the water became wine. God will take our water (prayers) and turn them into wine (answers), according to His infinite wisdom and love. Will you be like the obedient servants in selfless devotion to take your prayers to the Master?

READ AND TAKE NOTES:

Matthew 20:28

Galatians 5:13

Philippians 2:3-8

James 5:13-16

Talk to God about the beauty of service in prayer as it relates to your life:

Author EllynAnne Geisel writes in *The Apron Book*, "Wearing an apron is just good sense, especially in the kitchen. It's your armor against the splatter. It's your oven mitt, ingredient gatherer, jar opener, dishrag, counter wiper, window defogger, and smoke swatter at whatever moment you might need any one of these things. And when things go wrong—it'll dry your tears after a good cry. How do you get along in a kitchen without an apron? You don't."

I believe we can apply those literal uses of the apron in our earthly kitchen to our heavenly prayer kitchen. We can gather our ingredients in the Word, open the windows of heaven, put on our armor against the enemy, swat away the smoke of offense, defog our way to wisdom, wipe our sins away, let our tears be captured, and much more.

Don't you want to tie on your apron strings and enter the Kitchen of Prayer?

To help us delve into the "pots and pans" of the Kitchen of Prayer, I have devised an acronym using APRON to comprise the key ingredients. We will look at these in the following sections:

Adoration
Praise
Repentance
Offering of Thanks
Needs and Intercession

Included in each section is what I call your "Pantry Provisions," from the writings of Sylvia Gunter and used with her gracious blessing. I hope you will enjoy her rich resources long after you have completed this Bible study.

As you spend time with God, reading His Word and praying, perhaps start your own Pantry Provisions list as God lays things on your heart. I started one of my own when I saw a recurring theme of words beginning with "re" that contain wonderful spiritual riches. Here is what I have so far; please join me and add to it:

Rejoice in My Redeemer	Renewed
Rescued	Remembered
Redeemed	Refined
Restored	Removed my sins
Reconciled	

Remember, this acronym and the resources are tools and not dogmatic or magic formulas. They are designed in a way to help prepare our hearts and center our thoughts on Him. Each one reminds us to be humble and respectful of who He is and what He has done, is doing, and will do for us. I hope and pray they will be beneficial to you and that you will use them as ingredients to make your own unique "recipes of prayers" as you and the Lord communicate.

Be creative! In the back of the book (spiral-bound edition only) you will find a pocket folder with a few prayer cards to get you started. Perhaps find a cute recipe box with 3 x 5 cards to keep an account of your prayers, either alphabetically or topically, from the Pantry Provisions. Make your own lists. Record answers. Consider it your little treasure chest to preserve the faithfulness of our Father for future generations and to extol His goodness. Just as we read in Isaiah 63:7, let us also "tell of the kindnesses of the Lord, the deeds for which he is to be praised, according to all the Lord has done for us."

So, tie on your apron of prayer, pull up a chair to your kitchen table, and prepare to be fed!

An Apron for Every Season

Just as in the natural world, seasons come and go in our lives. They look and feel different. The appearance and utility of our "prayer aprons" will evolve and adapt as the seasons ebb and flow. You may be in a season of hard work and are wearing a white butcher's apron. It may carry the stains of being in the trenches. Your apron may have lots of pockets as you are carrying loads of responsibility. Perhaps a frilly organza signifies a time of hospitality and celebration for you.

God is the supreme designer of your apron, and you can trust that the design is fashioned out of His goodness and grace, His mercy and love. The end result will be nothing less than a personal masterpiece He sovereignly made for yet another masterpiece—you!

However, we have a responsibility to protect and care for our prayer aprons. The world, the flesh, and the devil would love to soil them, tear them, and rip them off.

Read: Philippians 4:6-8

Read: Colossians 3:12-14

List the ways you can Scotchgard® your apron.

Are you struggling with your apron during the season you're in right now?

READ: PHILIPPIANS 4:12-13

What is the antidote?

Take everything discussed in this lesson and sit with God at your kitchen table of prayer. (Isn't that where most of our best conversations take place?) Talk with Him about the masterpiece He is creating with your APRON of prayer.

ADORATION

ADORATION

God alone is worthy of our adoration simply for who He is. He is the great I AM. The King of Kings and the Lord of Lords. The Alpha and Omega. Omnipotent, omnipresent, and omniscient. He could be anything He wanted to be toward us. He could be distant and totally unapproachable. He could be aloof and arrogant. He could be a harsh taskmaster and unforgiving despot. But He is not. He is the total opposite. He is pure grace! He is pure love!

Richard Foster in his book, *Prayer: Finding the Heart's True Home*, states, "In adoration, we ask for nothing but to cherish Him. We seek nothing but His exaltation. We focus on nothing but His goodness." Spending time worshiping God in adoration is a beautiful way to come into His presence. "Awe-filled adoration," Tim Keller suggests, "sets the tone to correct the other forms of prayer."

The word origin of "adore" is from the Latin *adorare*. Ad = to and orare = pray, meaning "to pray, to worship, pay divine honors, bow down before." The heartbeat of prayer is adoration.

Adoration belongs to One. Too often adoration is exchanged with asking. Yet there is so much to adore about our Lord.

I struggle with speeding through "Adoration." Don't be discouraged if you feel like you aren't doing a good enough job here. It takes practice and discipline. I have a friend who is an only child whose parents doted on her. When we get together with our group of friends and the conversation strays too far and too long away from her, she busts in (jokingly, of course), and says, "Okay, back to me," and we all laugh because we love her (she really isn't self-centered). When I get off-track, straying too far and too long away from adoration, I say: "Okay, Lord, back to You." Sometimes I have to say it many times a day, and I sense His grace and love every time.

On a scale of 1-10, what is your "rush quotient" to get to the part in your prayers where you ask God for His help and provisions while skipping over His splendor and worthiness?

Talk to God about the number you wrote.

If your "rush quotient" is high, prayerfully write down some ideas to help you linger in adoration to our Lord.

Look at it this way. No one likes to be used. When someone asks us for things without acknowledging or respecting us, or investing in a relationship with us, we feel used and taken for granted.

Being appreciated for who we are and not just for what we can do not only nurtures a healthy relationship, but also makes us more willing to help.

> Are we Jesus-users or Jesus-adorers?
> –Ann Voskamp

Describe a time when you felt used.

What would have made the situation better?

How can you nurture a healthier relationship with God?

Worshiping God in adoration for who He is re-centers us in the reality that our almighty, loving, faithful, forgiving, gracious, and merciful God is on the Throne. Despite life's circumstances, He is good and trustworthy and worthy to be adored, magnified, and exalted for who He is. Don't overlook or skimp on the centrality of adoration.

Scripture is ripe with acclamations to God for His infinite greatness and His worthiness of our adoration. Let's focus on Psalm 145 with fresh eyes and list the attributes of our God who so deserves our humble and grateful adoration.

Does that illustrious list bring to mind a hymn or praise songs? Then sing! "O come let us adore Him…"

Traveling to Tuscany, Italy, for a once-in-a-lifetime vacation for my 50th birthday with my two daughters, sister, aunt, cousin, and friends was nothing short of spectacular, and I give God all the glory. Although the trip was to celebrate my milestone birthday, I didn't want that to be the focus. My heart longed for God to be glorified for His good gift and prayed for that to be so throughout the year of planning.

My sister, Kathy, and I live several states apart, but over the years she had become acquainted with my friends. The trip to Italy afforded my sister the opportunity to spend more time with my close friends. They knew of my deep desire for my sister to come to know Jesus Christ as her Savior and have a personal relationship with Him. My friend, Kay, was especially sensitive to this and prayed the whole week we were together for an opportunity to share the Gospel with her.

One day as our little bus roamed along ancient country roads of delightful scenery, our tour guide, Leo, a movie buff, asked if we would like to make an unscheduled stop at a monastery in which scenes from *The English Patient* were filmed. "Sure!" came the resounding chorus from the back of our bus. *La dolce vita!*

An avenue of regal cypresses stood guard as they guided us to the majestic sixteenth century monastery. Breathtaking frescoes dating from 1503 depicted the artist's rendering of Christ's life and drew us into the refectory. The long communal table centered the room with exquisitely carved benches hugging the walls.

The Holy Spirit moved among us as my friend, Lorri, spontaneously began singing praise to our Father. We stood or sat in reverential awe of the presence of God and His love for us. I looked over at my sister, Kathy, sitting on one of the benches and saw tears streaming down her face. My heart was full of gratitude for this extraordinary touch of His presence we shared in that room, but especially for my sister.

For our last night together in Italy, I planned a special worship service. Nestled in a medieval, fortified hamlet, an intimate twelfth-century chapel once again brought us to the majesty of the almighty and yet personal God as we sang and praised, prayed and acclaimed.

After we got back to our villa, Kay prayerfully went to see Kathy in her adjoining room. Kathy told her how she longed for what the rest of us enjoyed in our sweet, close-knit relationships. Kay shared that the sweetness and close connections were because of our common love for Jesus. Kay explained that we are all separated from God by our sins, but how God sent His Son, Jesus, to die a sacrificial death on the Cross to remove our sins and to restore us to our Maker.

By then Kathy was eager, by faith, to acknowledge Jesus as her Savior. She and Kay prayed and shed many happy tears. The next morning as we were packing to leave, my sister came into my room giddy with excitement. She could not wait to tell me her exciting news. Hallelujah! Praise and glory to God! I had been praying for my sister's salvation for 29 years. What an amazing birthday gift! Adoration and prayer opened heaven's gate for God's glory.

READ: PSALM 24 AND PSALM 100

Worship the King of glory with your own psalm of adoration and write it here:

Your Pantry Provisions for "Adoration" is a list of 365 names, titles, and attributes depicting who God is. He alone is worthy of adoration for every single one. Dig deeper into God's Word and excavate more with a word study, to expand your understanding about each one. Perhaps fill out a 3 x 5 card for your recipe box with what you learned. Magnify and adore Him every day of the year!

PANTRY PROVISIONS
A YEAR'S WORTH OF REASONS FOR ADORATION

Abba, Father
Abiding
Able
Abounding and Abundant
Adequacy
Adonai, Lord and Master
Advocate
All
All-knowing
All-powerful
Almighty God
Alpha and Omega
Amen
Ancient of Days
Anointed of God
Answer
Architect and Builder
Arm of the Lord
Ascended
Atonement
Author and Finisher of faith
Authority
Available
Avenger
Awesome
Balm of Gilead
Banner to the people
Beautiful
Before all things
Beginning and end
Beloved Son of God
Betrothed
Blameless
Blessed hope
Blesser
Bread from heaven
Bread of life
Bridegroom
Bright morning star
Brightness of glory of God
Brother
Burden-bearer
Captain of the Lord's host
Carpenter

Chief cornerstone
Chief shepherd
Child Jesus
Choice and precious
Chosen of God
Christ Jesus, our Lord
Christ, the power of God
Cleansing
Comforter
Coming again
Commander of the Army of the Lord
Compassionate
Complete
Confidence
Conquering
Consolation
Consuming fire
Counselor
Covenant-keeping God
Cover for sin
Creator
Crucified
Defender and defense
Deliverer
Desire of nations
Despised and rejected of men
Died and lives again

Discerner
Dominion
Door
Dwelling place
El Elyon – most high God
El Roi – God who sees
El Shaddai – all-sufficient
Elohim – eternal God
Endures
Enthroned
Eternal God
Eternal life
Ever-present
Everlasting Father
Everlasting name
Exalted
Excellent
Expected one
Faithful and true
Father of lights
Father of mercies
Father to the fatherless
First and the last
Firstborn of all creation
Forerunner
Forgiver of sin
Fortress
Foundation stone

Fountain for sin
Fragrance
Friend; friend of sinners
Full of grace and truth
Fullness
Generous
Gentle and kind
Gift of God
Giver of every good gift
Giver of life
Glorious Lord
Glory of Israel
God of all comfort
God of all grace
God of deliverances
God of glory
God of hope
God of Israel
God of love and peace
God of retribution
God of vengeance
God our Savior
God the Father
God who sees
Good shepherd
Goodness
Governor
Grace and gracious
Great
Great high priest
Guarantor of a better covenant
Guard and guardian of my soul
Guide
Head of every man
Head of the church
Healer
Hearer
Heavenly Father
Heir of all things
Help and helper
Hiding place
High and exalted one
Holy
Holy One of Israel
Holy Spirit
Hope
Horn of salvation
Humble
Husband
I AM
Image of God
Immanuel, God with us
Immortal
Incarnate

Incorruptible
Indwelling
Infinite
Inheritance
Innocent; sinless, perfect
Instructor
Intercessor
Jealous God
Jehovah-Jireh (Provider)
Jehovah-M'Kaddesh (Sanctifier)
Jehovah-Nissi (Banner)
Jehovah-Rohi (Shepherd)
Jehovah-Rophe (Healer)
Jehovah-Shalom (Peace)
Jehovah-Shammah (Ever present)
Jehovah-Tsidkenu (Righteousness)
Jesus
Jesus Christ, our Lord
Jesus of Nazareth
Jesus, the Son of God
Joy
Judge of the earth
Just One and Justifier
Keeper
King eternal
King of glory
King of Israel
King of kings
King of the Jews
Lamb of God
Lamp
Lawgiver
Liberty
Life and life-giving spirit
Light
Light of revelation
Light of the nations
Light of the world
Lily of the valleys
Lion of Judah
Living bread
Living God
Living water; unfailing spring
Long-suffering
Lord God, the Almighty
Lord Jesus Christ
Lord of all
Lord of glory
Lord of hosts
Lord of lords
Lord of the harvest
Lord of the Sabbath
Love and loving

Lover of my soul
Lovingkindness
Lowly in heart
Magnificent
Maker
Majesty; majestic glory
Man Jesus Christ
Man of sorrows
Man whom God appointed
Marred, pierced, stricken, rejected
Marvelous
Mediator
Meek
Merciful
Messiah
Mighty God
Morning Star
Most High God
Nailed to a cross
Name above all names
Near
Never-failing
New Covenant of God
None other
Obedient Son
Offering for sin
Omnipotent

Omnipresent
Omniscient
On high forever
Only begotten Son
Only God, our Savior
Only one
Only wise God
Over all
Overcomer
Paraclete
Pardoner
Passover, blood of the Lamb
Patient
Peace
Perfect
Physician
Portion
Potter
Power and wisdom of God
Precious cornerstone
Priest
Prince of peace
Prophet
Propitiation for our sins
Protector
Provider
Pure
Purifier

Quieter of the storm
Quick and powerful Word of God
Quickener
Rabboni
Radiance of His glory
Ransom
Reconciliation
Redeemer
Refiner
Refining fire
Refuge
Reigns
Rescuer
Restorer of my soul
Resurrection and the life
Revelation
Reviving One
Rewarder and reward
Righteous judge
Righteous One
Righteousness
Risen Lord
Rock of refuge and strength
Rock of salvation
Root and offspring of David
Rose of Sharon
Ruler

Salvation
Same
Sanctification
Sanctuary
Satisfaction
Scepter
Searer of hearts and minds
Security
Seed of Abraham
Seeker
Sent
Servant of God
Shade
Shadow of the Almighty
Shelter
Shepherd
Shield
Sin-in-bearing sacrifice
Slow to anger
Son of David
Son of God
Son of Man
Son of righteousness
Son of the Highest
Song
Source
Sovereign
Spirit of adoption

Spirit of counsel and power	Understanding
Spirit of God	Uniter
Spirit of grace	Unsearchable
Spirit of holiness	Unspeakable gift
Spirit of the Father	Upholder of all things
Spirit of the Lord	Upright One
Spirit of truth	Vengeance
Spotless; unblemished	Very present help
Stay	Victor
Steadfast	Victorious warrior
Strong deliverer	Vindicator
Stronghold	Vine and vinedresser
Suffering servant	Voice of the Lord
Sufficient	Wall of fire
Sun and shield	Way
Sun of righteousness	Witness to the peoples
Sure, and our surety	Wonderful Counselor
Sustainer	Word of God
Teacher from God	Word of life
Tower of strength	Worker of wonders
True God	Worthy
True light	Yesterday and forever the same
True riches	
Trustworthy	Zealous
Truth	Zion's righteous King
Unchanging	

Used with permission from *Prayer Portions* by Sylvia Gunter

DINING WITH JESUS
THE ALABASTER JAR OF ADORATION

READ: LUKE 7:36-50

Who invited Jesus to dinner and what was His response?

What does this tell you about Jesus?

Describe the woman who showed up at the dinner uninvited and what she brought. (vs. 37)

What did she do and what did her actions show?

What did the Pharisees' actions (or lack thereof) show?

What did Jesus's response show?

Is there any pharisaical behavior (contempt, judgment, disbelief) that you relate to?

How well do you relate to the woman who was unabashedly brave, totally repentant, and fervent in her love toward Jesus?

Talk to God about your answers.

Would you like to bring your own alabaster jar of adoration to Jesus? What's in it? Break it open and imagine the pleasing fragrance, while you tell Him the reasons you adore Him.

INSPIRATION APRON
PRAYER AND PERSEVERANCE

Susanna Wesley (1669-1752) was a woman of great faith and unequivocally committed to glorifying God. She understood the importance of prayer and is known for using her apron while she prayed. A hardworking mother of ten children (she gave birth to nineteen; however, nine died in infancy) kept her very busy, but she made sure she took time to pray. The story goes that when she lifted her apron over her head, her children knew not to disturb her because she was praying.

Many challenges filled Susanna's life including chronic sickness and harsh poverty. With her husband absent for long periods, because of marital strife and debtors' prison, Susanna bravely carried on. She did so, despite two suspicious house fires that almost cost her son, John, his life, a crop fire, and the malicious slitting of their cow's udder to destroy the family's milk supply.

Susanna's dedication to God and her family remained unwavering. As the primary source of her children's education, both secular and spiritual, Susanna spent innumerable hours in this endeavor. She, however, always made sure she spent one hour a week with each child one-on-one.

Two of her children, John Wesley and Charles Wesley,

impacted Christendom in remarkable and far-reaching ways, bringing glory to God and building His Kingdom. John touched nearly a million lives proclaiming the Good News of salvation through Jesus Christ, while shepherding a great spiritual awakening in England, which resulted in the founding of the Methodist Church. Charles's fervent love for God led him to pen over 9,000 hymns such as "Christ the Lord is Risen Today" and "Hark, the Herald Angels Sing."

Susanna is quoted as saying, "I am content to fill a little space if God be glorified."

Write: 1 Corinthians 10:31

Write: 1 Peter 4:11

Spend some time talking with God about "your space" and "His glory."

As a disciple of Jesus, jot down some ideas you can implement that would glorify God.

John Wesley said of his mother, "I have learned more about Christianity from my mother than all the theologians in England."

Prayerfully consider those in your life you would like to tell about Christ.

What are your favorite attributes about Christ that you would share?

PRAISE

PRAISE

Perhaps adoration and praise blend together for you, blurring any distinction between the two. This quote by Charles Spurgeon resonates with me, reminding me that *adoration tunes our praise instruments*. "When we come to praise, we should not rush into our praises helter-skelter, but engage in them with prepared hearts. I notice that when musicians are about to perform, they tune their instruments. There is also a preparation of themselves in rehearsals before they perform their music in public. In the same way, our souls ought to rehearse the subject for which they are about to bless God."

Now let's consider who God is *for* us and prepare to be blessed! Our God is totally approachable and closer than our next breath. He is caring and humble. He is our all-wise God and forgiving Lord. His goodness and mercy follow us all the days of our lives and we will dwell in His house forever (Psalm 23:6). I believe that is my favorite verse as it doesn't get any better than that!

He is worthy of our praise for who He is to us and for us. Praise not only glorifies the One to whom all praise is due, but it also builds our faith, our love for God, and our hope in Him. It opens wide the windows of heaven to pour out the abundant, joy-filled life He died for us to have while protecting us from the evil one. Let the music begin!

Write: Isaiah 43:21

Write: 1 Peter 2:9

Write: Psalm 29:2

Write: Psalm 113:3

Write: Hebrews 13:15

READ: PSALM 63:1-8

READ: PSALM 103:1-5

Rejoice in those words of truth and, in your own vernacular, join with the saints of the ages. As David says in Psalm 34:1, "I will extol the Lord at all times; his praise will always be on my lips." Do the same and give praise to God for who He is to you.

READ: LUKE 19:37-40

Are there any areas in your life that the stones will cry out because of your lack of praise? Harry Ironside, pastor and author, said, "We would worry less if we praised more." Raise your hand if you want to worry less. Now keep your hand up in praise and raise your heart and voice in worship to Him, letting go of your worries.

I tend to hang on to things out of sentimentality. I have years, uh…decades of greeting cards and thank-you notes from family and friends. I keep them because I love the ones who gave them to me, and their words are meaningful. They represent their love for me. In the same way, our praises are meaningful to God. He keeps and treasures each one of our "notes" of love and praise to Him.

READ: REVELATION 5:8

What did John see the four living creatures and twenty-four elders carrying and what did they hold?

What is the word between "which" and "the?"

Yes, *are*—present tense!

Your prayers are so important to God that He keeps them

in beautiful bowls, and they *are* ever before Him. They are the very air God breathes!

Write God a note of praise for the immense privilege of prayer and the wonderful knowledge that your prayers live in the Throne Room with Him as a pleasing aroma.

Now jot down a fresh, new prayer to add to God's golden bowl.

On a trip to Turkey, I purchased a small red-and-blue geometric rug with braided tassels on two sides. I was told it was most likely made and used by a nomadic tribe. One day after I returned home, I hung it outside to air it out, and an unexpected rain shower dampened it. When I rushed to bring the rug inside, an exquisite bouquet of exotic spices rose to greet me. The fragrance delighted my senses and transported me back to the beauty and mystery of Turkey.

Praise is the "spice" of prayer. It transports us to the Throne Room, with all its mystery and beauty, bringing a lovely aroma to the One alone who deserves to be magnified and honored for what He means to us.

Spices and their blends are limitless. So, too, our "spice blends" of praise.

What creative combination do you want to concoct today for your spice jar of praise?

Use the Pantry Provisions that follow (study the provided scriptures) and fill God's heavenly incense bowls with the pleasing scent of your praises. Let's join with King David to resolve to praise God *more* and *more* (see Psalm 71:14).

PANTRY PROVISIONS
OVER 100 REASONS TO PRAISE

My Abba-Father, my Papa God – Mark 14:36, Romans 8:15, Galatians 4:6

My all-able, almighty God – 2 Corinthians 9:8, Ephesians 3:20, Revelation 4:8, 19:6

My all-knowing (wisdom) – John 21:17, 1 Corinthians 1:30

My all-sufficiency (all-sufficient) – 2 Corinthians 3:5, 12:9-10

My alpha and omega, beginning and end – Revelation 1:8, 21:6, 22:13

My answer – Jeremiah 33:3, Psalm 20:1, 6, 9

My authority – Matthew 28:18, John 17:2

My banner of victory – 1 Corinthians 15:57, Proverbs 21:31, Zephaniah 3:17, 1 Chronicles 29:11

My beautiful Lord and King – Psalm 27:4, Isaiah 33:17

My holder together-er – Colossians 1:17, Romans 11:36

My breach-mender – Isaiah 58:12, Romans 5:10-11, Ephesians 2:16, Colossians 1:20-22, 2 Corinthians 5:18-19

My burden-bearer – Psalm 55:22, 68:19, 1 Peter 5:7

My cleansing – 1 John 1:7, 9, Isaiah 1:8

My comforter – 2 Corinthians 1:4-5, Psalm 23:4

My compassion and grace – Lamentations 3:22, Exodus 34:6, Psalm 103:8, 111:4, 116:5, 145:8

My confidence, unshakable – Psalm 71:5, Proverbs 3:26, 14:26,

Hebrews 4:16, 1 John 5:14

My cornerstone and sure foundation – Isaiah 28:16, 33:6, 1 Corinthians 3:11, Ephesians 2:20

My counselor, my friend – John 14:26, Isaiah 11:2, John 15:14-15, Luke 7:34

My covenant-keeping God – Deuteronomy 7:9, Malachi 2:5, Hebrews 8:6

My creator – Genesis 1:1, 1 Peter 4:19

My defender and defense – 1 John 2:1, Proverbs 23:11, Jeremiah 50:34

My deliverer – Psalm 18:2, 144:2

My desire, more precious than silver – Isaiah 26:8, Proverbs 3:13-15, Psalm 73:25-26

My Emmanuel, ever-present with me, available, near – Matthew 1:23, Psalm 139:7, Acts 17:27

My endurance and encouragement – Romans 15:4-5, Philippians 2:1, Hebrews 6:18, Daniel 6:26, Psalm 112:3, 9

My everlasting I AM – Exodus 3:14, John 8:58, Psalm 106:48

My exalted One – Psalm 18:46, 97:9, 148:13, Acts 2:33, 5:31

My faithful and true God; trustworthy – Revelation 19:11, 2 Timothy 2:13, 1 Thessalonians 5:24

My Father – Deuteronomy 32:6, Psalm 68:5, Isaiah 9:6, Matthew 5:48, 1 John 1:3, 3:1

My forgiveness of sin; my pardon – Ephesians 1:7, Colossians 1:14, Isaiah 55:7, Micah 7:18

My fortress and stronghold – Psalm 9:9, 31:2-3, 62:6, Jeremiah 6:19, Proverbs 14:26

My fullness, filling all things – Colossians 1:9-10, Ephesians 1:23

My gentleness and kindness – 2 Corinthians 10:1, Titus 3:4

My giver of every good gift – James 1:17, Romans 8:32, Luke 11:13

My giver of life – John 5:21, Romans 4:17

My glory – Psalm 3:3, Hebrews 2:7, John 1:14

My God of miracles who works wonders for me – Psalm 72:18, Isaiah 25:1, Galatians 3:5

My God who is always there – John 20:28, Revelation 21:7, Psalm 63:1, Ezekiel 48:35

My good shepherd, good to me – John 10:11, 14, Psalm 34:10, 85:12, 119:68

My grace and truth – John 1:14, 17, Ephesians 2:7

My great and awesome God – Exodus 15:11, Psalm 99:3

My guide and the way – Psalm 16:8, 48:14, 73:24, John 14:6, Hebrews 10:20

My head of the church – Ephesians 1:22, 4:15, 5:23, Colossians 1:18

My healer – Exodus 15:26, Psalm 103:3

My heart surgeon – Psalm 51:10, Jeremiah 24:7, Ezekiel 11:19, 36:26

My help, very present – Hebrews 13:6, Psalm 46:1

My hiding place – Psalm 32:7, Isaiah 4:6

My holy, holy, holy God – Isaiah 6:3, Revelation 4:8

My Holy Spirit – Acts 2:28-29, John 1:33, 14:26

My hope – Colossians 1:27, 1 Timothy 1:1

My "I AM" in all things – Exodus 3:14-15, Psalm 119:91,

Romans 8:28

My jealous God – Exodus 34:14, Joshua 24:19

My joy and song – John 15:11, Romans 14:17, Psalm 40:8

My judge of all the earth – Acts 10:42, 17:31, 2 Timothy 4:1, 8, Revelation 19:11

My justification – Romans 5:18, 8:23

My keeper – Psalm 121:5, Isaiah 26:3

My King of glory – Psalm 24:7-10, 1 Corinthians 2:8

My King of kings on His throne – 1 Timothy 6:15, Revelation 19:16

My lamp; my light – 2 Samuel 22:29, Psalm 18:28, 27:1, Micah 7:8

My liberty – 2 Corinthians 3:17, John 8:32, Galatians 5:1

My life – 1 John 5:1, John 11:25, Colossians 3:4

My living bread; living water – John 4:10, 6:51, 7:37-38, Revelation 22:17

My living God, living in me – Psalm 42:2, Romans 8:11, Isaiah 12:3

My Lord of all – Acts 10:36, Romans 10:12

My love; lover of my soul – Micah 7:8, Romans 8:35-39, 1 John 3:1

My majestic God – Psalm 93:1, Hebrews 1:3

My marvelous One – Revelations 15:3, Job 37:5

My master – Colossians 4:1, 2 Timothy 2:21

My merciful and compassionate God – Deuteronomy 4:31, Luke 1:78, 1 Peter 1:3, Lamentations 3:22, Exodus 34:6

My most high God – Psalm 78:35, Acts 16:17, Mark 5:7

My name above all names – Philippians 2:9, Ephesians 1:21

My never-failing God – Hebrews 13:5, Deuteronomy 31:6, 10
My none other – 2 Samuel 7:22, Isaiah 45:21
My One whom I adore – Song of Solomon 1:4, Jeremiah 31:3, Hosea 11:4
My overcomer; over all – Romans 9:5, John 16:33
My patient God, long-suffering, slow to anger with me – Romans 2:4, Psalm 103:8, 145:8
My peace – Ephesians 2:14, Philippians 4:7
My perfection; perfect – Hebrews 2:10, 7:28
My portion; all I need – Psalm 16:5, 73:28, Lamentations 3:24, Colossians 3:11b
My potter – Isaiah 64:8, Jeremiah 18:6
My precious God – Isaiah 28:16, 1 Peter 1:19, 2 Peter 1:4
My provider; my source – Philippians 4:19, Psalm 34:10, 84:11
My redeemer – Job 19:25, Psalm 19:14
My refiner; purifier; consuming fire – Malachi 3:2-3, 1 John 1:7, Hebrews 12:29, 1 Corinthians 3:13
My refuge – Psalm 46:1, 91:2, 4, Deuteronomy 33:27
My restorer of my soul – Isaiah 57:18, Psalm 23:3, Joel 2:25
My reviver – Psalm 19:7, 80:18, 85:6, Isaiah 57:15
My rewarder and my reward – Hebrews 11:4, Revelation 22:12, Isaiah 40:10
My riches, true – Romans 9:23, 11:33, Ephesians 1:7, 18, 2:7
My righteousness – Jeremiah 23:6, 1 Corinthians 1:30
My rock – Psalm 31:2-3, 144:1, 1 Corinthians 10:4
My salvation – Habakkuk 3:18, Luke 1:47, 2:11, 30, Revelation 19:1

My satisfaction – Psalm 17:15, 36:8, 63:5, 103:5, Isaiah 58:11, Matthew 5:6

My searcher of my heart – Psalm 139:1, 23, 1 Chronicles 28:9, Revelation 2:23

My security, stability, and stay – Proverbs 14:26, Deuteronomy 33:12, Psalm 18:8

My shade; my shelter – Psalm 5:11, 61:4, 63:7, 91:1, 121:5, Isaiah 25:4

My shield and protector – Psalm 91:4, Proverbs 30:5, John 17:11

My sovereign God – Daniel 4:35, Psalm 103:19, Habakkuk 3:19

My spirit of truth – John 14:17, 16:13

My steadfast and sure God – Psalm 19:9, 111:8

My strength – Psalm 18:1, 59:9-10a, 17, Isaiah 12:2, Ephesians 1:19, Philippians 4:13

My sustainer – Psalm 55:22, 89:21, Isaiah 46:4, Ruth 4:15, Hebrews 1:3

My teacher – John 13:13, Isaiah 28:6, Psalm 32:8

My tower, strong – Psalm 61:3, Proverbs 18:10

My unchanging God; the same yesterday, today, and forever – Hebrews 13:8, Malachi 3:6, Psalm 102:27, James 1:17

My understanding – Psalm 147:5, Jeremiah 9:24, Isaiah 11:2, 40:28, Ephesians 1:8

My vine, my abiding place – John 15:1, 5

My worthy One to be praised – Revelation 4:11, 5:12, Psalm 18:3

Used with permission from *Prayer Portions* by Sylvia Gunter

DINING WITH JESUS
THE BREAKING OF BREAD

READ: LUKE 24:13-35

What did Cleopas and his companion ask Jesus? (vs. 29)

In what manner did they ask? (vs. 29)

What was Jesus's response? (vs. 30)

    I *love* that Jesus agreed to stay with them! Jesus had a lot of places to go and people to see. After all, it was the first day of His resurrection!

    He loved Cleopas and his friend and wanted to share

Himself with them while feeding them the truth of who He is. The never-changing Jesus wants to do the same for you and me. Spending time at the table with Jesus makes Him happy and opens our spiritual eyes.

When was the last time you asked Jesus to spend time with you? Invite Jesus to dinner in your heart. What does He want you to see? Ask Him. Write down the impressions you receive.

INSPIRATION APRON
DO THE NEXT THING

From a remote jungle in Ecuador, Elisabeth Elliot was thrust into the limelight in 1958 when *Life* magazine published a ten-page spread about the five American missionaries speared to death by men of the Auca tribe. One of those men was Elisabeth's husband of three years, Jim Elliot, and Elisabeth became a young widow and single mother to baby daughter, Valerie.

The story doesn't end there, however. Elisabeth not only continued to serve in Ecuador with the Quechua people, but also met two Auca women who lived with her for a year. Those women were the entryway for Elisabeth and her daughter to live with the Auca for two years, despite their extremely primitive and notoriously violent ways. Through witnessing the love, grace, and forgiveness Elisabeth exhibited, the Auca tribe came to faith in Jesus Christ as their Savior. The Aucas, which means "savage" are now called Waodani, "the true people." One tribe member believes if they had not put their faith in Jesus, there would be none of them left.

Elisabeth and her daughter eventually returned to the United States, and she became a popular author and speaker. Her books continue to inspire. She remarried in 1969, but sadly, Addison Leitch died of cancer after only four years of marriage.

Although not looking to marry again, God had other plans. She married Lars Gren four years later in 1977. She preceded Lars to heaven in 2015 at the age of 88.

I had the privilege of hearing Elisabeth speak in 1990, and my most profound takeaway is one I still adhere to today and pray for others to do the same: "Do the next thing." Elisabeth spoke of being confused and uncertain in the jungle without her husband. All she wanted to do was collapse in a heap and feel sorry for herself. Instead she trusted God and did the next thing.

She gleaned the wise principle from an old Saxon poem:

> From an old English parsonage down by the sea
> There came in the twilight a message to me;
> Its quaint Saxon legend, deeply engraven,
> Hath, as it seems to me, teaching from Heaven
> And on through the hours the quiet words ring
> Like a low inspiration: DO THE NEXT THING.
> Many a questioning, many a fear,
> Many a doubt, hath its quieting here.
> Moment by moment let down from Heaven,
> Time, opportunity, guidance are given.
> Fear not tomorrows, child of the King,
> Trust them with Jesus. DO THE NEXT THING.
> Do it immediately; do it with prayer;
> Do it reliantly, casting all care;
> Do it with reverence, tracing His hand
> Who placed it before thee with earnest command,
> Stayed on Omnipotence, safe 'neath His wing,
> Leave all resultings. DO THE NEXT THING.

Looking to Jesus, ever serener,
Working or suffering be thy demeanor;
In His dear presence, the rest of His calm,
The light of His countenance be thy psalm,
Strong in His faithfulness, praise and sing!
Then, as He beckons thee, DO THE NEXT THING.

–Emily Elizabeth Steele Elliott
English author, editor, and hymnist
(1836-1897)

What is your next thing?

Although Elisabeth's physical presence has left us, her books and radio show, "Gateway to Joy," remain. They continue to point people to Jesus, teaching joyous living no matter the circumstances, by trusting in God's character and not the outcome.

Elisabeth believed and lived her words:

> Everything if given to God can become your gateway to joy.

What do you need to give to God to become your gateway to joy? Write your thoughts and turn them into a prayer.

Elisabeth began her radio show by saying, "You are loved with an everlasting love. That's what the Bible says, and underneath are the everlasting arms."

Write: Jeremiah 31:3

Write: Deuteronomy 33:27

Praise God for His love and His everlasting arms, and perhaps illustrate your words.

REPENTANCE

REPENTANCE

I get moths in my food pantry from time to time. They can be difficult to exterminate. No matter how clean and careful I try to be, they creep in. Those buggers are persistent and pesky.

I can take a paper towel and crush each moth as I see it, which is fine and good, but I must get to the root of the problem in order to get rid of them. We must do the same with our sin. We can crush each sin with our confession, which again is good and also critical, but we must repent to get to the root of the problem.

READ: SONG OF SOLOMON 2:15

We may not have "little foxes" in our vineyards, but we have "little moths" in our pantries.

Here is the extermination procedure to get rid of these pests:

- ❖ Realize we've done something wrong and acknowledge our sin
- ❖ Feel sorrow, regret, and contrition for our action
- ❖ Confess our wrongdoing to God and, if needed, to those who were hurt
- ❖ Change our mind about our behavior – hunger and thirst after righteousness and you will be satisfied (Matthew 5:6)
- ❖ Dedicate ourselves to changing – for it is God who

works in you to will and to act according to His good purpose (Philippians 2:13)
- ❖ Abide in Jesus and have His words abide in you (John 15:7)

This is not a white-knuckle, do-it-yourself job. This is allowing the Holy Spirit to renew us day by day (2 Corinthians 4:16).

As sincere followers of Christ, our earnest desire every day is to "Love the Lord your God with all your heart and with all your soul and with all your mind…and love your neighbor as yourself" (Matthew 22:37, 39). Sin (remember our old buddy, "self"?) is like the bully in elementary school that wheedles his way to the front of the line and pushes love to the back of the line. Be an impregnable "Line Leader." Daily tell the Lord, "Create in me a pure heart, O God, and renew a steadfast spirit within me" (Psalm 51:10). Tell Him now.

One of the best weapons I use to get rid of my pantry moths are lures I purchased from Amazon that attract them to a sticky surface. We, too, have a lure that conquers the pest of sin: God's Word.

READ: PSALM 119:9-16

READ: 2 TIMOTHY 3:16-17

In your own words, agree with the psalmist and Timothy regarding the importance of feeding on God's Word and keeping His commandments:

Another remedy I use for moths is vinegar. In ancient times vinegar was used as medicine and as a germ killer. As far back as 400 BC, Hippocrates, known as "the father of medicine," used vinegar to treat his patients.

In John 19:29-30 we read: A jar of wine vinegar was there, so they soaked a sponge in it, put the sponge on a stalk of the hyssop plant, and lifted it to Jesus' lips. When He had received the drink, Jesus said, "It is finished." With that, he bowed His head and gave up His spirit.

Let's use the vinegar of confession and repentance as an antiseptic to wipe away our sins.

Billy Graham put it this way: "The wonderful news is that our Lord is a God of mercy, and He responds to repentance." So, my friend, run to Him—not away from Him—despite any embarrassment or discouragement. You are His, and He holds you with complete security in His compassionate love.

If we confess our sins, He is faithful and just and will forgive us our sins and purify us from all unrighteousness (1 John 1:9).

It is finished, indeed!

Repentance means we want a clean pantry more than we want the sin. We can sometimes hold on to sins almost as "pets" because we are comfortable with them, and they make us feel good—short term. It's like eating the food you don't need when you'd like to lose a few pounds. But don't we all want clean pantries? To lose a few pounds?

Using the Pantry Provisions for Repentance, allow the Holy Spirit to prompt you in the extermination process. Perhaps use a 3 x 5 card from your "prayer recipe box," and jot down scriptures and prayers for each of the categories and sub-categories. If there are any sins that you need to confess time and time again, spend as much time as you need to deep clean the nooks and crannies of the pantry of your heart to eradicate the contamination.

Read: Psalm 51

Read it again, and after each time you spend in repentance, join David in a wondrous journey of God's divine forgiveness, love, and acceptance. Echo David's sentiments in your own words.

Read: Psalm 32:1-2

Thank God for this amazing blessing of forgiveness!

READ: ISAIAH 44:22

Now, I want you to go outside if it's a pretty day with clouds and be like a little kid again. (If weather does not permit today, make sure you do it another day.) Grab a blanket, lie on your back, and gaze at the clouds. If you aren't able to lie on your back, that's okay; just watch intently. As the clouds migrate across the sky and make their exodus to who knows where, embrace afresh the wonder of your redemption. Write or sketch about it here.

Write: Romans 8:1

Thank God anew for His marvelous promise and what it means to you personally.

PANTRY PROVISIONS
REASONS TO REPENT

ANGER (Dishonoring God's Love and Forgiveness)
- Bitterness
- Resentment
- Unforgiveness
- Revenge
- Hurts
- Keeping accounts
- Impatience

PRIDE (Dishonoring God's Grace)
- Cold heart/cold love
- Critical spirit
- Judgment
- Envy
- Jealousy
- Murmuring and complaining
- No servant spirit
- Offending others
- Being opinionated
- Stubbornness

SELF (Dishonoring God's Lordship)
- Selfishness, self-centeredness
- Self-pity
- Self-justification

- Defending my rights
- Striving with God (struggling against)
- Being a spiritually spoiled child
- Unkindness
- Unloving attitude or actions
- Insensitivity
- Impatience

NO FEAR OF GOD (Dishonoring God's Holiness)

- Disobedience
- Compromise; tolerance of evil
- Idols of the heart: family, time, self, job, leisure, comfort, etc.
- Busyness
- Laziness; idleness; undisciplined life
- Loss of first love for Jesus
- Little prayer
- Not knowing God through His Word
- Not needing discipline by God
- Not keeping God's day holy
- People-pleasing more than God
- No concern for the lost
- Misuse of the tongue
- Gossip
- Pet sins
- Procrastination

CONTROL (Dishonoring God's Sovereignty)

- Expectations that are not God-given
- Demanding rights
- Independent spirit
- Manipulation
- Perfectionism

LUST (Dishonoring God's Righteousness)
- Coveting a person sexually
- Sexual indulgence
- Love for things of this world
- Divided heart: eternal values vs. world's values
- Gluttony, addiction to anything: food, television, pleasure, reading, sports, alcohol, drugs

LYING (Dishonoring God's Truth)
- Falseness; pretense
- Deception
- Untruth

UNBELIEF (Dishonoring God's Word)
- Fear–"What if…"
- Guilt
- Living by feelings
- No joy
- Depression
- Hopelessness
- Tension
- Anxiety
- Worry

Used with permission from *Prayer Portions* by Sylvia Gunter

DINING WITH JESUS
BREAKFAST ON THE BEACH

Are you tired? Work fatigued without reward? Discouraged? Burdened? Grieving? Crushed? Perplexed or frustrated with life's circumstances and fretting about where they might be taking you?

You are not alone. Jesus's disciples felt all the above. All their hopes and plans and dreams were dashed when Jesus died on the Cross. Jesus loved them unconditionally, cared for them deeply, and gave them purpose and hope for the future. The disciples poured everything they had into following Jesus, and then He was gone. Confused and heartbroken, they picked themselves up by their sandal straps and did not wallow in their despair. They put one foot in front of the other, launched their boat into the water, and pressed on.

But they were not abandoned. Someone was right there caring for them and helping them. The same is true for you.

READ: JOHN 21

Jesus's compassion, love, provision, and encouragement oozed all over the beach that morning. Nothing had changed with Jesus. Nothing has changed.

What did Jesus call the disciples? (vs. 5)

After they caught the fish, what did Jesus want them to do? (vs. 12)

Jesus wanted to share a meal with His friends and talk to them about important things, such as Peter's restoration after his denial blunder. He reminded them to "Follow Me" and reprimanded them, if put in today's vernacular, "to mind their own business."

"Come and have breakfast," Jesus said.

Jesus wants to have breakfast with you, too, my friend. He has important things to tell you. Be still. Listen. What is He saying? Write it down.

INSPIRATION APRON
SURRENDER AND SERVICE

Ida Scudder's father and grandfather served as medical missionaries in India. Ida spent her young childhood there witnessing the horrors of famine, which left her with indelible, unpleasant memories—and a determination to never return after her education was finished in the United States. In fact, when her school friends teased her about it, she vehemently replied through tears that she would never, never, *never* return to India.

However, in 1890, not long after graduating from the Northfield Seminary for Young Ladies in Massachusetts, her mother became ill, and Ida was summoned to help care for her. Vowing to return to America as soon as her mother's health permitted, she reluctantly boarded a ship to India.

One quiet evening at her parents' home, she sat writing a letter to her friend telling her she was not suited for missionary life; she looked forward to returning to America. Over the course of that same evening, not one, not two, but three different knocks at the front door altered her plans as God ordered her steps in a totally different direction.

The three knocks were from first a Brahmin, then another high-caste Hindu, and finally a Muslim, all pleading for Ida to help their wives in difficult childbirths. With no medical training, she instead offered the services of her physician father. All three refused his assistance because their religious beliefs and cultural customs prohibited such contact.

Tears and agony were Ida's companions that night as she wrestled with God, in anguish over the fate of the women—and her own—as she knew God was directing her to a path she did not want to take. Early the next morning, the haunting sound of tom-tom drums and the wails of mourners confirmed that all three young women lost their lives because no man other than their family could look upon them.

After much thought and prayer, Ida's "never" became null and void. She would go back to America not to become a wife and mother as she had dreamed, but to become a medical doctor and help the women of India.

Returning to Vellore, India, with her medical degree and a generous donation, Ida was able to open a hospital, a medical school for women (eventually becoming co-ed), and a nursing school, as well as an orphanage and a mobile clinic. She devoted herself in sharing the Gospel, praying with patients, answering their questions about Jesus and Christianity, and teaching the Bible. Ida's dream was not to build a medical school, but the Kingdom of God.

Fast forward over one hundred years and Dr. Ida Scudder's legacy includes a medical complex that is one of the largest in Asia, where chapel services are given in eleven languages. Millions of patients have benefited physically. Thousands of doctors and nurses have been trained there, while affording many of them and their families the opportunity to leave behind a life of poverty.

Ida Scudder lived her motto: "not to be ministered unto but to minister." In 1960 this servant of God died in India at age 89. Her gravesite, where a life-size photo of Ida adorns her tomb, is always arrayed with fresh flowers.

Write: Galatians 2:20

Write: Romans 12:1

READ: MARK 8:34-35
What did Jesus say we must do?

READ: JOSHUA 24:14-15

Write down any idols that are keeping you from faithfully serving God.

READ: PROVERBS 3:5-6

READ: PSALM 143:8

What should we be doing?

What should we not be doing?

What is the result if we adhere to trusting God?

Did Ida's story resonate with you? Has there been a time in your life when you made your plans, but God ordered your steps (Proverbs 16:9) in a significant way? What have you learned? Is there anything else you would like to learn through this? Have you talked to God about these things? Now is a good time.

Do you actively seek God's will? Do you ask Him what it is? Or are you wandering about in your own little world? Do you give God's world precedence? "But seek first His Kingdom and His righteousness, and all these things will be given to you as well" (Matthew 6:33). Respond here in prayer, but more important, stop and listen for the answers. Therein lies the feast of life.

Do you have a "never" that could be keeping you from God's best? Talk to God about it.

Ida's vision and mission for her life's work was, "We seek to be a witness to the healing ministry of Christ through excellence in education, service, and research."

Think about the ministry of Christ that Jesus has for your life. Have a heart-to-heart staff meeting with your "boss," the Lord of your life. Take notes.

OFFERING OF THANKS

Offering of Thanks

I cringe at the thought and am horrified to admit to myself and to you, but I have caught myself with the attitude of, "What have you done for me lately, Lord?" Ugh. Ouch. Yuck! As I type this, I am heartsick and sorrowful.

If Jesus did not do another thing for me, what He has already done through His sacrificial, shed blood on the Cross for my sins is enough. More than enough. Infinitely enough. And, I didn't even deserve that. Amazing grace, indeed! Jesus + nothing = everything.

Read: Psalm 107

The psalmist begins and ends extolling God's love and goodness and then offering his own thankfulness. Did you catch the pattern in the middle as the psalmist recounts God's help to His people time and again, over many situations and crises? The Israelites were in trouble, they prayed to the Lord for deliverance, and He answered them by bringing them out of their distress. Have you been led out of a desert? Has something imprisoned you of which you are now free? Have you been healed from a sickness? Have you been rescued from a storm? Has God been gracious and merciful to you?

Take a few minutes to remember and recount, and then give thanks for what God has done in your life. Choose and write your own personal life verses of thanks for God's goodness and love to you.

READ: PSALM 66

Look at verse 17 again. In addition to his cries, what did the psalmist do?

If you are currently in a desert, prison, sickness, or storm, don't give up crying out to the Lord. Also, don't forget to thank Him. His love endures forever. His answer is coming. He is the same yesterday, today, and forever (Hebrews 13:8). As He helped the Israelites, so will He help you.

Jesus gave His ALL that we may have ALL, and we do!

Everything we are, everything we have, and everything we are able to do is because He allowed it in His sovereignty, mercy, and lavish love. Giving Him thanks should always be at the forefront of our hearts.

Write: 2 Peter 1:3

God has given us life, and He could have stopped there. But He gives us everything else pertaining to living a godly life.

Continue reading in 2 Peter 1:4-11. What are some ways we can show our thanks based on these scriptures?

Write: Psalm 9:1-2

Write: Colossians 3:17

Right now, give thanks with all your heart. Tell of God's wonderful deeds to your circle of influence and to those who cross your path. Social media is a fabulous place with a wide audience for us to bear witness to a dying world of the living God's magnificence and love for all of us. Rejoice and be glad as you remember and recite who God is and what He means to you. Sing a song of praise.

Write: James 1:17

Write: Ephesians 5:20

Thank God for the good gifts He has given you. Write a few of them here:

Write: Colossians 4:2

Write: 1 Thessalonians 5:18

Take a moment to thank God for a circumstance that is troubling you. Write your thanksgiving here and then ask Him two questions: How do You want me to grow? What do You want me to learn through this?

Write: 1 Peter 5:7

In prayer, cast your anxiety on Him and thank Him for caring for you.

Read: Psalm 136

Join with the psalmist in agreement and personally give thanks to God here:

The Pantry Provisions for "Offering of Thanks" is a compilation of who we are in Christ. Our finite minds cannot grasp the infinite goodness and gifts God has bestowed upon us. But we must try! Let's cook up some fantastic recipes of thanksgiving using these marvelous "ingredients."

PANTRY PROVISIONS
AN ALPHABET SOUP OF THANKSGIVING

Able to do all things – Philippians 4:13
Abounding in grace – 2 Corinthians 9:8
Abounding in hope – Romans 15:4, 13
Abraham's offspring – Galatians 3:29
Accepted – Romans 15:7
Adequate – 2 Corinthians 3:5
Adopted – Galatians 4:5
Adversary of the devil – 1 Peter 5:8
Alien and stranger in the world – 1 Peter 2:11
Alive with Christ – Galatians 2:20
Ambassador for Christ – 2 Corinthians 5:20
Anointed – 1 John 2:27
Anxious for nothing – Philippians 4:6
Appointed by God – John 15:16
Assured of reward – 1 Corinthians 15:58
Assured of success in Him – Proverbs 16:3
Baptized into Christ – Romans 6:3
Beautiful – Isaiah 61:10
Becoming a mature person – Ephesians 4:13
Becoming conformed to Christ – Romans 8:29
Belonging to God – John 17:9
Blameless at His coming – 1 Thessalonians 5:23

Blessed – Jeremiah 17:7
Blessed with spiritual blessing – Ephesians 1:3
Bold and confident – Ephesians 2:18, 3:12
Bond-servant – Psalm 116:16
Born again – 1 Peter 2:5
Born of God – 1 John 5:18
Buried with Christ through baptism – Romans 6:4
Called – 1 Corinthians 1:9
Cared for with compassion – 1 Peter 5:7
Carried – Exodus 19:4
Cherished – Ephesians 5:29
Child of God – John 1:12
Chosen – Colossians 3:12
Christ is my hope – Colossians 1:27
Christ is my life – Colossians 3:4
Circumcised spiritually – Colossians 2:11
Citizen of heaven – Philippians 3:20
Clay in the Potter's hand – Jeremiah 18:6
Clean – John 15:3
Cleansed – 1 John 1:7, 9
Clothed with Christ – Galatians 3:27
Comforted – 2 Corinthians 1:4-5
Complete in Christ – Colossians 2:10
Confident – Proverbs 3:26
Confident He will finish me – Philippians 1:6
Confident He will never leave me – Hebrews 13:5-6
Confident of answers to prayers – 1 John 5:14-15
Conformed to His image – Romans 8:29

Conqueror, more than – Romans 8:37
Continually with God – Psalm 73:23
Controlled by the love of Christ – 2 Corinthians 5:14
Created in Christ for good works – Ephesians 2:10
Crucified with Him – Galatians 2:20
Dead to sin, alive to God – Romans 6:6, 11
Delighted in – Isaiah 42:1
Delivered – 2 Timothy 4:18
Desired – Psalm 45:11
Died and my life hidden in God – Colossians 3:3
Disciple of God – Luke 9:23
Disciplined – Hebrews 12:5-11
Drawing near with confidence – Hebrews 4:16
Empowered to obey – Philippians 2:13
Encouraged – 2 Thessalonians 2:16-17
Enlightened – Ephesians 1:18
Enriched in everything – 1 Corinthians 1:5
Equipped – 2 Timothy 3:17
Eternal life – Romans 6:23
Every good thing, having – Philemon 1:6
Eyes fixed on Jesus – Hebrews 12:2
Favored – Psalm 5:12
Fearing God – Psalm 25:14
Fellow citizen with the saints – Ephesians 2:19
Filled with the fullness of God – Colossians 2:9-10; Ephesians 3:19
Filled with the full measure of His joy – John 17:13
Filled with the knowledge of His will – Colossians 1:9

Filled with the fruit of righteousness – Philippians 1:11
Filled with the fruit of the Spirit – Galatians 5:22-23
Finished product in progress – Philippians 1:6
Forgiven of my sins – 1 John 1:9
Formed from the womb – Jeremiah 1:5
Fragrance of His knowledge – 2 Corinthians 2:14-15
Free – Romans 8:2
Freed from sin – Romans 6:7, 22
Friend of God – John 15:14-15
Fruit-bearer – John 15:5, 16
Future assured – Romans 8:18, 28
Gifted – Romans 12:6
Given all things – Romans 8:32
Given His magnificent promises – 2 Peter 1:3-4
Given the Holy Spirit as pledge – 2 Corinthians 1:22
God is for me – Romans 8:31
God's gift to Christ – John 17:24
Granted grace in Christ Jesus – Romans 5:17, 20
Guarded by God – 2 Timothy 1:12
Guarded by God's peace – Philippians 4:7
Guided – Psalm 48:14
Heir – Galatians 3:29, 4:7
Helped by Him – Isaiah 44:2
Hidden with Christ in God – Colossians 3:3
His – Isaiah 43:1
His handiwork – Ephesians 2:10
Holy – Hebrews 10:10
Holy and blameless – Ephesians 1:4

Holy and dearly loved – Colossians 3:12
Honored – 2 Timothy 2:21
Hope fixed – Romans 15:4, 13
Image and glory of God – 1 Corinthians 11:7
In Christ Jesus – 1 Corinthians 1:30
Indestructible – 1 Peter 1:23
Indwelt by Christ Jesus – John 14:20
Indwelt by His Spirit – Romans 8:11
Inscribed on His palms – Isaiah 49:16
Inseparable from His love – Romans 8:35
Instrument of righteousness – Romans 6:13
Joint heir with Christ – Romans 8:17
Justified – 1 Corinthians 6:11
Kept – 1 Peter 1:5
Kingdom of priests – Revelation 1:6
Knowing all things work for good – Romans 8:28
Knowing whom I believe – 2 Timothy 1:12
Known – 2 Timothy 2:19
Lacking no wisdom – James 1:5
Lavished with riches of His grace – Ephesians 1:7-8
Laying aside the old self – Ephesians 4:22-24
Led in Christ's triumph – 2 Corinthians 2:14
Life abundant – 1 John 4:9; John 10:10
Life and peace in the Spirit – Romans 8:6
Light, having – John 8:12
Light of the world – Matthew 5:14
Like a watered garden – Isaiah 58:11
Living Christ's life – Galatians 2:20

Living for Him – 2 Corinthians 5:15
Living stone – 1 Peter 2:5
Lord's, the – Isaiah 44:5
Loved constantly, unconditionally – Isaiah 43:4
Lover – Psalm 18:1
Made alive with Christ – Ephesians 2:5
Made by Him – Psalm 100:3
Member of His body – 1 Corinthians 12:27
Mind of Christ, having the – 1 Corinthians 2:16
Minister of reconciliation – 2 Corinthians 5:18-19
Named – Isaiah 43:1
Near to God – Ephesians 2:13
Need met by His riches, my – Philippians 4:19
Never forsaken – Hebrews 13:5
New creation – 2 Corinthians 5:17
New life – Romans 6:4
New self – Ephesians 4:22-24
No condemnation – Romans 8:1
No fear – John 14:1, 27
No longer children – Ephesians 4:14-15
No longer slaves to sin – Romans 6:6
Not given a spirit of fear – 2 Timothy 1:7
Not my own – 1 Corinthians 6:19
Noticed with loving concern – Psalm 33:13-14
Object of mercy – Romans 9:23
Obtained an inheritance – Ephesians 1:11
Of God's household – Ephesians 2:19
On the winning side – Colossians 2:15

One spirit with Him – 1 Corinthians 6:17
One with Him – John 17:23-24
Overcomer – 1 John 5:4-5
Partaker of Christ – Hebrews 3:14
Partaker of grace – Philippians 1:7
Partaker of the divine nature – 2 Peter 1:4
Partaker of the promise in Christ – Ephesians 3:6
Peace with God, having – Romans 5:1
People, His – 2 Corinthians 6:16
Pilgrim and stranger – Hebrews 11:13
Possession, His special – 1 Peter 1:18-19
Power of God behind me – Philippians 3:21
Prayed for – Luke 22:32
Prayers, go up before God – Revelation 8:4
Predestined and adopted – Ephesians 1:5, 11
Prepared beforehand for glory – Romans 9:23
Presented to God holy, blameless – Colossians 1:22
Pressing forward – Philippians 3:14
Priest – 1 Peter 2:9
Protected – 2 Thessalonians 3:3
Provided for – Matthew 6:33
Purchased – Revelation 5:9
Purposeful – Psalm 138:8
Qualified to share His inheritance – Colossians 1:12
Raised up with Christ – Ephesians 2:6
Received an unshakable kingdom – Hebrews 12:28
Received mercy – 1 Peter 2:10
Received the riches of grace – Ephesians 1:7

Received the Spirit from God – 1 Corinthians 2:12
Redeemed – Galatians 3:13
Refined – 1 Peter 1:6-7
Reigning in life – Romans 5:17
Rejoicing – Romans 5:2-3
Renewed – 2 Corinthians 4:16
Representative, His – Matthew 5:16
Rest, provided – Matthew 11:28-30
Revelation, having from God – 1 Corinthians 2:10, 12
Rewarded by God – Isaiah 49:4
Rich – 2 Corinthians 8:9
Righteous – Romans 3:22, 26
Righteousness of God – 2 Corinthians 5:21
Rooted and built up in Him – Colossians 2:7
Royalty – Romans 5:17, 8:16-17
Royal priesthood – 1 Peter 2:9
Safe – Psalm 4:8
Saint – Romans 1:7
Salt of the earth – Matthew 5:13
Sanctified – 1 Thessalonians 5:23
Seated in heavenly places – Ephesians 2:6
Secure – Deuteronomy 33:12
Sent – John 20:21
Servant, His – Romans 6:22
Set free – John 8:31-32, 36
Sharing Christ's inheritance – Romans 8:17
Sharing His glory – John 17:22, 24
Slave of righteousness – Romans 6:18

Sheep, His – Psalm 23:1
Soldier – 2 Timothy 2:3-4
Son of God – Romans 8:14
Spirit of love, power, sound mind – 2 Timothy 1:7
Stable – Isaiah 33:6
Standing firm in Christ – 2 Corinthians 1:21
Steps established by the Lord – Psalm 37:23
Strengthened in Him – Ephesians 3:16
Strong in the Lord – Ephesians 6:10
Sustained from birth – Psalm 71:6
Sweet aroma of God – 2 Corinthians 2:14-15
Temple of the living God – 2 Corinthians 3:16, 6:19
Thought about – Psalm 139:17-18
Transferred to kingdom of His Son – Colossians 1:13
Transformed into His image – 2 Corinthians 3:18
Treasured – Psalm 83:3 (NASB)
Truth – John 17:7
Unafraid – Isaiah 44:2, 51:12
Understanding things given by God – 1 Corinthians 2:12
Understood – Ephesians 1:8 (TLB)
United with Christ – Romans 6:5
Unworthy – 1 Corinthians 4:7
Upheld – Deuteronomy 1:30-31, 33:27
Useful for His glory – Isaiah 43:7
Valued – Matthew 6:26
Victorious – 1 Corinthians 15:57
Waiting for our Savior – Titus 2:13
Walking in new life – Romans 6:4

Walking worthy of God's calling – Ephesians 4:1
Washed – 1 Corinthians 6:11
Wisdom – Colossians 2:3
Witness, His – Acts 1:8
Worshipper, His – Psalm 95:6
Yielded to God – Romans 6:13

Used with permission from *Prayer Portions* by Sylvia Gunter

DINING WITH JESUS
THE JOY OF SITTING AT HIS FEET

READ: LUKE 10:38-42

Just as Martha opened her home to Jesus, we have opened our hearts to Him. But then Martha became busy and distracted. Sound familiar? Is your heart too busy and distracted for Jesus? Jesus used Martha's name twice because she was deeply entrenched in things the Lord deemed unnecessary, and she was doing them with the wrong heart attitude.

What things are distracting you?

Are they necessary?

Are you doing things with a bad attitude?

Write vs. 41 substituting your name:

The Lord already knows what has you worried and upset. What are they? Talk to Him about them.

Instead, what does the Lord want? (vss. 39, 42)

Sit at the Lord's feet and listen to what He says. Put pen to paper.

INSPIRATION APRON
LOVE FOR JESUS AND OTHERS

When I travel, many of my photos lean toward older women going about their day. I especially love Italian women. Perhaps my affinity began as a child, since the town I grew up in, with its large Italian population, gave me many friends of Italian descent. I loved their exotic last names that rolled off my tongue, their love for *famiglia,* and their delicious food and hospitality. Italian women are loving, funny, wise, warm, and interesting. They are also fabulous cooks with servant hearts and feisty personalities (think on the order of Sophia Petrillo in *The Golden Girls,* except not as outrageous.)

So when I heard about Molly Bruno, I had to investigate.

If you are familiar with the movie *War Room,* the character of Miss Clara, the prayer warrior, was based on Molly Bruno. A New Yorker from Staten Island, Molly loved Jesus with all her heart and, thus, loved people. Her heart's desire was for everyone she met to know Jesus as their Savior.

Her daily, fervent prayer was, "Lord, please send someone across my path today I can talk to about You."

And did she ever! Countless times, resulting in remarkable stories. I will recount just a few from the book, *The Audacious*

Molly Bruno, written by her daughter, Marie Armenia, who has gladly given her permission.

Molly loved the New York Yankees and received as a rare treat free tickets to a game. During the game a woman in her section caught a fly ball that jammed her ring into her finger. When she cried out in extreme pain, Molly went over and sat with her to comfort her while the paramedics cut off her ring.

Dismissing the fact that she was missing the uncommon opportunity to watch a Yankees game live, Molly continued to sit with the stranger. The woman thanked her but wanted to know why she was being so kind. Molly replied in Molly fashion, "I wanted to help you. And now that you feel better, I want to tell you that Jesus loves you." The woman was hungry for the truth Molly shared with her, and Molly rejoiced as the woman bowed her head and prayed for Jesus to be her Savior and Lord—at Yankee Stadium!

Molly stood waiting at a bank one day in a very long line of fifty deep. A foul-smelling woman entered and made a disruptive commotion with her loud tirade of obscenities about the long line. Everyone ignored her, except Molly, whose heart went out to this woman who appeared to be a drug addict and prostitute. Molly offered her a place in front of her in line. No one had been kind to Monya in years, and she was baffled as to this silver-haired lady's kindness to her. Monya asked, "Why did you let me get in front of you?"

Molly smiled. "So I could tell you Jesus loves you."

Monya retorted that she was beyond anyone loving her. Molly explained that God is real and that He loved her. Monya challenged her. "Well, if God is real, then tell Him to let me find my daughter." Skeptical, but magnetized by Molly's words, Monya gave Molly her phone number and address and asked her to pray that she would find her daughter. A few days later, much to Monya's surprise, the silver-haired lady from the bank showed up at her door. Monya received Christ in faith through Molly's visit that day.

Molly brought Monya some new clothes, and Monya attended church with her new friend and sister-in-Christ. Shortly thereafter, when Monya heard about a faith-based drug recovery program in the Bronx, she entered it. After being there for only one week and while attending a Bible study, Monya heard a man speak about his uncle. His very unusual name led to the discovery that the man he described was *her* uncle, as well. Through this miraculous encounter with a distant relative she'd never met before, Monya was joyfully reunited with her daughter!

On yet another day, Molly and her husband, Joe, were driving across the Staten Island Outerbridge, when the traffic came to a screeching halt. A man had jumped off the bridge in a suicide attempt. Molly was the first to spot him after he miraculously survived and was swimming toward a concrete column. Frantic over the dire situation, Molly cupped her hands and screamed at the top of her lungs, "JESUS LOVES YOU!"

Amazingly, he answered from the dark and dirty water approximately fifteen stories below and yelled, "I NEED JESUS! WILL HE HELP ME?" Molly reassured him that she was sure He would, as well as forgive all his sins no matter how egregious.

On a bridge 135 feet above murky waters, Molly heard the man crying out to God for mercy and forgiveness. The man was rescued both from the river and hell. God forgave him, but the state of New York saw to it that he was punished for his previous crimes. He is now serving a life sentence in prison and leading others to know the same Jesus who had rescued him.

Molly was a beautiful, shining light who reflected the God she loved. She loved people and wanted everyone to know the same brilliant Light she knew, the One who pours out forgiveness and captures hearts with His love.

In 2015, Molly saw that Light face-to-face at age 92.

READ: MATTHEW 22:34-39

Write Jesus's first and second commandment.

Take a few moments and reflect anew upon the first commandment and write a love note to God.

What neighbor is God laying on your heart? Ask God how you can love that neighbor and then write out a plan of action.

Think about Molly and pray to be ready to share Jesus and His love with the ones who cross your path today.

NEEDS AND INTERCESSIONS

NEEDS AND INTERCESSIONS

Finally! Did you think we would ever get to praying for our personal needs and for the needs of others (intercession)?

God hears all of our prayers, no matter the order. However, using the APRON acronym helps to anchor us in the Truth. It allows us time to get "self" off center stage and for the spotlight to shine on God, His Word, and His will—for His glory and our good. It enables the natural to align with the supernatural, for He is the ultimate Source who owns all resources.

The world God created for us went from total perfection to total imperfection—from us having no needs to needing everything. And yet, wondrously, God in His love and grace still faithfully supplies everything we need. No need is too small or too great in God's listening ears. Just as a child tells a parent, a friend tells a friend, a wife tells her husband, a patient tells the doctor, a student tells the teacher, and a customer tells the clerk what they need to get that need met, we too, must be dedicated and fervent in telling the ultimate Supplier. For it is our sovereign Father who meets all of our needs. He may use the parent, the spouse, the doctor, the teacher, or the clerk, but God is the utmost Source. It is important we tell Him what we need.

My friend, Cyndee, traveled to Swaziland on a mission

trip. On the last day, she and her friend decided not to spend it sightseeing, but to visit one more village. They went to the local grocer and bought all the one-pound bags of rice on the store shelves. They hiked up and down rolling hills, handing out the bags of rice to the villagers. At their very last stop of the day, they arrived at a typical homestead, which consisted of about a dozen children, three ladies, and a very elderly grandmother, known as a gogo. They worked in the garden with them, played with them, and prayed with them.

After they started down the hill to return to their hotel, Cyndee remembered the last bag of rice in her backpack. She ran back up to the elderly gogo and placed the bag of rice in her hands. Breaking into a huge, mostly toothless grin, the jubilant woman started whooping and hollering and broke into a full-on "happy dance." When she caught her breath, she explained her outburst of pure joy. She simply said, "I have been praying all day long for a cup of rice." Hallelujah, God answers our prayers and supplies our needs!

Write: Philippians 4:19

Who?

Will do what?

How many?

How does this get accomplished?

Write: 2 Corinthians 9:8

Rewrite this scripture in your own words as a prayer to God.

Write: Psalm 84:11-12

What does God give?

To whom?

Who are blameless and blessed?

In days gone by, the main use of aprons was for carrying everything from eggs in the henhouse to vegetables from the garden, from apples in the orchard to logs from the woodpile. Aprons held an abundance.

Martin Luther, the father of the Reformation, spent many hours in prayer, believing prayer was the utmost work. "As is the business of tailors to make clothes and cobblers to make shoes, so it is the business of Christians to pray," Luther said.

God wants us to share our needs and concerns through prayer, Luther concedes, "not because He is unaware of them, but in order that we may kindle our hearts to stronger and greater desires and spread our aprons wide to receive many things."

Jesus has the power. Jesus *is* the power. When we bring Him our needs in prayer, we release His power.

Read: Matthew 7:7-11

Hold open your apron and tell our Father what you need.
Hold open your apron and ask your Father to help others.

We have all been in difficult situations (or will be) when friends and family ask, "What can I do for you?" The answer we give most often is, "Pray." Charles Spurgeon believed, "No man can do a truer kindness in this world than pray for me." I'm sure we all agree. And, may I add, there's no truer help in this world than prayer.

I know the prayers spoken in intercession on my behalf during hardships gave me strength to endure. I envision those precious and mighty intercessors raising my arms for the trial as Aaron and Hur held up Moses's arms to fight the battle (Exodus 17:8-16).

We see the importance throughout Scripture of the need and power of prayer for others. A few examples: Abraham for Sodom (Genesis 18); Moses for the Hebrews (Exodus 32); Paul as he prayed unceasingly for the early church (Ephesians 1), and, of course, Jesus. He prayed for His disciples, He prayed for us in John 17, He prayed on the Cross, and He is praying NOW.

Author Richard Foster says, "If we truly love people, we will desire for them far more than it is within our power to give them, and this will lead us to prayer: Intercession is a way of loving others."

Some members of our church did that one evening as we gathered for an emergency prayer meeting for our precious friend and sister, Luc. She was to undergo a second heart surgery.

This is her account of what happened:

> As I sat in a chair in our living room with hands laid on me, and these dear ones beseeched God on my behalf, I gave over the dread of being cracked open and missing a tremendous family reunion. Of course, there were prayers for peace, comfort, traveling mercies, wisdom and skill for the doctors, and easy recuperation. Then our new co-pastor, a man who devoted his heart and soul to seeking the Lord, prayed as best I can remember—"Lord, you say we have not because we ask not. So, I am going to boldly ask that You help Luc and Bob have a nice drive tomorrow to North Carolina, and that when they meet with the doctor, he will tell them that she does not have to have surgery, then please give them a nice leisurely drive back to Atlanta."
>
> I slept well that night. On the eight-hour

drive, I reread my journal from the first surgery, grateful I had forgotten the pain and process, even though I still felt so held in the Lord's arms—then and now.

The next morning as we prepared to finalize our plans with the surgeon, some oversights in the original doctor's office arose. All the preliminary tests and procedures had to be redone for the surgeon to be able to look at what was going on with my heart. The tests were redone and we waited for the doctor to review the newly done tests and procedures. I remember remarking how I felt the best I had in months, and how odd it was that the next day I had open heart surgery scheduled!

Then the doctor entered the office with a smile on his face. "Luc doesn't need surgery."

The problem was not there anymore. My heart had been miraculously healed!

My heart was leaping and dancing. Hallelujah!

The Lord is my strength and my shield; my heart trusts in him, and he helps me. My heart leaps for joy, and with my song I will praise him (Psalm 28:7).

We drove back to Atlanta, just as our pastor had prayed.

We were able to attend our family celebration. It was wonderful, memorable, and heart-filled.

On a follow-up echocardiogram the following week, my cardiologist who originally saw the problem said, "This isn't the heart I saw a few weeks ago."

I will give thanks to you, Lord, with all of my heart; I will tell of your wonderful deeds (Psalm 9:1).

With God all things are possible! Just pray.

Read: Matthew 6:25-34

What does God know?

What does He want us to do?

What does He want us not to do?

READ: PSALM 55:22

Prayerfully tell God about your needs and worries. Prayerfully declare His promises. Write them here.

Remember our Executive Chef? He is wearing the most beautiful white chef coat imaginable. Just as the woman who suffered from bleeding touched His cloak in faith for her need, you also can touch the Executive Chef's coat in the Kitchen of Prayer for your need.

READ: MARK 5:24-34

Can you relate to the woman and her suffering and desperation?

Are you ready to cut through the throngs, whatever they look like in your life, in order to touch His garment? Name the things holding you back.

Now reach out in faith and have a heart-to-heart with God about the whole truth (Mark 5:28, 33). Pour it out here.

You are His precious daughter. Go to Him for healing, peace, and freedom from your suffering (Mark 5:34).

READ: JEREMIAH 29:13

READ: EXODUS 34:29

READ: PSALM 34:5

What will happen when we seek God with our whole heart?

When we seek someone, it is because we want to be with them and talk with them. We have something to say to them, and we know they have something to say to us. God is our constant Companion, and whether connecting with Him during a dedicated time alone or on-the-fly, His Presence and power are always with us. We have to appropriate His Presence and power by consciously seeking Him with devotion throughout the day. Seeking is praying. He is our best resource, because He is our source.

Talk to God about seeking Him, His Kingdom, and His righteousness—and the promise that follows.

God is our "I AM" for every need and every situation: spiritually, physically, mentally, and emotionally. Jesus is the Answer. Using the Pantry Provisions, beautifully knead your needs and intercessions for others with the Bread of Life. Search the scriptures that back up these truths and pray them. A sweet aroma will rise to the Throne Room.

We may not be able to travel to Swaziland or other locales around the world, but our prayers can still bring a bag of rice to those in need. Ask God for His provisions.

Don't give up. The gogo did not give up. Neither should we.

Read: Luke 18:1-7

Read: Luke 11:5-10

Don't look at the injustices or circumstances that are happening in your life and the world but, instead, look to Jesus. Be the persistent widow and pesky neighbor, just like the gogo.

What have you given up praying for?

Renew your persistence and peskiness here.

But what about those times when there are no words, only tears? As Charles Spurgeon coined it, they are "liquid prayers," dear ones. We see in Psalm 6:8 that the Lord hears the voice of your weeping, and that your tears are valuable enough to Him that He stores them (Psalm 56:8).

Jesus weeps with us and for us. Our sorrow is Jesus's sorrow. His compassion and mercy never fail. Take a few minutes here and thank God that your precious tears are seen and are priceless to Him.

READ: JOHN 11:1-45

What did the weeping of Mary and her friends stir in Jesus? (vss. 33, 35)

Yet despite His tears, He did not languish there for long. He prays and He acts. His actions are both in the supernatural realm (praying) and physical realm (removing the stone and calling Lazarus forth). Let this be an example for us. As worthy as our tears are, be careful not to let feelings and circumstances cause stagnation. As we read in Elisabeth Elliot's story, "Do the next thing."

Using Jesus's example, how can you pray and what action can you take despite your tears?

Hang out in the Pantry Provisions and feast on God's storehouse.

PANTRY PROVISIONS
OUR GOD SUPPLIES OUR EVERY NEED

Abba Father – when we need fathering
Acceptance – when we feel unwanted
Adequacy – for our inadequacy
All-sufficient – in our hardest situations
Amen, true witness – when we are tempted to lie
Answer – for our uncertainty and questions
Author of our faith – for our unbelief or doubt
Before all things – when we're surprised
Bread of life – for our spiritual hunger
Bridegroom – when we need companionship and cherishing
Bright morning star – for the darkness in the valley of the shadow
Broken and spilled out for us – when we've been used
Burden bearer – when we are heavy laden
Cleansing – for our defilement and shame
Closer than a brother – when we are lonely
Comforter who wipes away tears – in our griefs and sorrows
Defender – when we are under attack
Deliverer; liberty – for our bondage or captivity
Door-opener – when it looks like there is no way out
Faithful friend – when friends fail us
Foundation, sure; solid rock – when we are shaking and insecure

Fullness – when we are empty
God of details – when we are frustrated
God of love – when we feel unloved and need a hug
God who is there – when we feel alone or abandoned
Grace – when we're too hard on ourselves and others
Guide; way – when we're confused and need direction
Healer – for our woundedness, rejection, physical illness
Hope – when we despair, are discouraged, and want to quit
Humility – for our pride
Joy – when we are depressed
Keeper and protector – when we are vulnerable
Lifter of our heads – when we feel oppressed and weighed down
Living water – when we are thirsty
Long-suffering; slow to anger – when we have blown it again
Mercy – for criticism and unkindness
Mighty God; our strength – for our weakness or temptation
Never-failing; the same – when we are fickle or faithless
Overcoming victory – for defeat and depression
Plumb line – to stand against the world's situational ethics
Prince of Peace – when we are stressed, worried, and confused
Provider – for every financial need
Quieter of the storm – for afflictions without and struggles within
Reconciliation – for breaches in relationships
Rest – when we are tired and can't go on
Restorer of our soul – when we are bruised and beaten down
Reviver – when we are depleted
Satisfaction – when we've tried everything and come up empty

Tie on Your Apron in the Kitchen of Prayer

Song, praise, psalm – when we are joyless and heavy of heart
Spirit of the Lord – when we need to be set free
Strength – when we are weak
Trinity; unity – for mending separation
True riches – when we're tempted to covet the world's wealth
Truth – when we've been lied to
Vengeance is the Lord's – when we are angry or wronged
Wisdom – for our hard choices

Used with permission from *Prayer Portions* by Sylvia Gunter

DINING WITH JESUS
FEEDING THE MASSES

Other than the resurrection, the miracle feeding of the masses is the only other story recorded in all four Gospels.

READ: MATTHEW 14:13-21

MARK 6:30-44

LUKE 9:10-17

JOHN 6:1-14

Imagine yourself on a crowded hillside, thankful that the relentless heat of the day is beginning to wane with the sinking of the sun into the horizon. You are tired and hungry but so utterly mesmerized by a man who is speaking straight to your heart, with such piercing love and authority, you cannot tear yourself away. Your stomach rumbles and growls, and yet you are filled with a joy and peace you have never felt before as you feed on the words this man, Jesus, is speaking. You don't want to leave His presence.

Besides that, He just healed you from an ailment. The pain is gone! You are deeply grateful and in awe of His power and compassion.

Jesus didn't want to "break up the party" either. Despite

His weariness and His grief (He had just lost His beloved cousin and friend, John the Baptist), His love and tenderness prevailed.

He wants to dine with His followers…including you. If you were the only person on that hillside, He would not turn you away.

He cares for you.

He knows what you need, and He supplies it.

And, there is plenty left over.

Remember a time when Jesus healed you and thank Him.

Talk to God about a time when His words fed your soul.

Praise God as you ponder the compassion He has for you.

Write a note of thanksgiving to God for supplying the needs you have.

What happened when Jesus thanked God for the two fish and five loaves?

Write a note of gratitude for God's multiplication in your life.

What happened after everyone was fed? (John 6:12-13)

God didn't want anything wasted.

According to dictionary.com, one of the definitions of waste, as a verb, is "to fail or neglect to use: to waste an opportunity."

My grandmother did not waste anything. She grew up in a home where frugality was a virtue. As a young mother, she raised her children during the Great Depression. She became a single mother in the 1940s. Those life experiences imprinted on her the motto of "waste not, want not." She saved every piece of string, sewing notion, used wrapping paper (you never knew how your next gift from her would be adorned), and every bit of salvageable food.

In the '60s and '70s, restaurants used a sprig of parsley as a popular garnish to enhance the dinner presentation. Although meant to be eaten after the meal as a breath freshener, few people partook. When we would dine out on an occasional Tuesday night, my grandmother's night off, she would gather everyone's parsley, which would inevitably end up in the diner's next day's soup.

All ketchup bottles were turned upside down for as long as it took to catch every drop, which would later be used in meatloaf. When my cousins, siblings, and I were children, she would fill our orange juice or milk glass only half full. Heaven forbid that we would be served more than we could drink and waste a drop! She would remind us that we could always have more.

Grandmom went to live with my aunt after she retired. Family pitched in and cleaned out her house before the move, and we found sack after sack of filled vacuum cleaner bags in the basement. When asked what she was saving them for, she said, "Well, I was going to go through them in case I had sucked up a back to an earring."

Although she instilled in me the beauty of prudent consumption, I often fail at wise conservation. I cringe at the food I've wasted, which under her watchful eye would have been met with her clucking tongue. But her unconditional love would have prevailed.

We know God isn't clucking His tongue at us as there is no condemnation in Christ Jesus, and He loves us unconditionally. But are we wanting things and yet wasting the opportunities He already has given us, particularly the privilege and blessing of prayer? The Word tells us in 2 Peter 1:3, "His divine power has given us everything we need for a godly life through our knowledge of him who called us by his own glory and goodness."

We've already discussed the importance of prayer for a godly life. Are you squandering or utilizing the immense privilege and power that we have been given in prayer?

Ponder your wastefulness and have a heart-to-heart with God. Write your conversation here.

INSPIRATION APRON
GOD DELIGHTS IN YOU

YOU!!!

Yes, you!

You are made in God's image, "fearfully and wonderfully made" (Psalm 139:14). There is no one like you, and you are extraordinary because, remember, the perfect Creator of the world, who doesn't make anything mediocre, created you! God delights in you. He has ordained your life and your days. Whether your days consist of a smile to one other person or a speech to hundreds, the value is the same because you are God's chosen vessel. Comparing ourselves to others negates God's sovereignty and deflates our spirits. Stop it. Please, please, please know who you are and that you are enough.

Let's look at scripture that details how wonderful we are in God's eyes. But first a quote comes to mind from a book popularized by the movie with the same name, *The Help*. Abilene, the maid and caregiver of the children of the house, tells her charge, "You is smart. You is kind. You is important." Then she has the child slowly repeat it back to her for reinforcement, to help the little girl believe those words.

We, too, need God to remind us of who we are in Him. And His truth reinforces the strong bulwark needed against the world, the devil, and even ourselves—all trying as often as possible to tell us otherwise.

As a child and young adult, I suffered from low self-esteem. This led to an embarrassing blushing problem. The unwanted invasion of scarlet upon my fair skin came easily and often because of my feelings of inadequacy and inferiority. I felt I was unworthy of any attention given to me. As I grew in the knowledge and acceptance of God's love for me, and as I learned how valued I am through Christ, the blushing decreased significantly. As I write this, I cannot even think of the last time I blushed, even when I've done public speaking (which isn't my favorite thing).

Our God has allowed us to see our value and worth through His Word and through His death on the Cross. His promises always prove true. When lies or negative feelings override God's truth, do this: stop, drop, and roll. Stop the thought, drop the lie, and roll the scripture off your tongue that counters the enemy's attack.

I repeat: no comparing allowed! Just as God made us individual and unique, so, too, are our gifts, our paths, our stories, and our legacies. All we need is to keep our eyes on Him in trust and obedience.

Read: Proverbs 3:5-6

Rewrite those verses in your own words and talk to God about them.

READ: EPHESIANS 1

What has God our Father and the Lord Jesus Christ given you? (vs. 2)

What has God and the Father of our Lord Jesus Christ blessed you with? (vs. 3)

What has God chosen you to be in Him before the creation of the world? (vs. 4)

What did He predestine in love for you through Christ Jesus? (vs. 5)

What did that bring Him? (vs. 5)

What has He freely given you? (vs. 6)

And what is the result? (vs. 6)

In Him, what else do you have and what has He lavished on you? (vss.7-8)

What has God made known to you? (vs. 9)

In what manner did He do so? (vss. 8-9)

For what purpose did He do this for you and for Him? (vs. 10)

According to God's plan, why were you chosen? (vss. 11-12)

When you believed, what did you receive and what was accomplished? (vss. 13-14)

What does Paul pray that the eyes of your heart be enlightened to know? (vss. 18-19)

Describe this strength you were given. (vss. 19-23)

READ: EPHESIANS 2

Why and what did God do for you? (vss. 4-5)

What else did God do for you and why? (vss. 6-7)

Explain in your own words the gift from God you received. (vss. 8-9)

Who are you? (vs. 10)

Why were you created in Christ Jesus? (vs. 10)

Where are you and how? (vs. 13)

What does being in Christ give you? (vs. 14)

Through Him, what access do you have? (vs. 18)

Who are you not? (vs. 19)

Who are you? (vs. 19)

READ: EPHESIANS 3

From this description, describe God's love for you in word or sketch. (vss. 17-19)

Express by word or illustration the power that is at work within you. (vs. 20)

Why were you given the power? (vs. 21)

Based on all of this knowledge—so much in just three chapters!—interpret in your own vocabulary what this means *for* you. In the form of a prayer, paraphrase what these truths mean *to* you.

What jumped out at you and why?

Focusing on your answer, what do you think God is saying to you?

Look at Ephesians 2:10 in several translations. Write down your favorite version and pray through it using "I" and your name.

Our Apron Jubilee

Prayers do not die. The lips that utter them may close in death, or the heart that felt them may cease to beat, but the prayer lives before God and God's heart is set on them. Prayers outlive the lives of those who utter them. Outlive a generation, outlive an age, outlive a world.

– E. M. Bounds

When we are absent from our bodies and at home with the Lord, precious women, we will hang our aprons of prayer on the eternal clothesline. Together, we'll watch them dance in the gentle breeze of the Holy Spirit as far as the eye can see, twirling about with…

> every acclamation proclaimed,
> every hallelujah shouted,
> every sin confessed and thrown into the
> Sea of Forgetfulness,

every sigh of gratitude,
every whisper spoken in the night,
every tear of liquid intercession gathered in God's bottle,
and every wordless groan.

Envision it all now. The spic-and-span fabrics sway gloriously, having been washed in the cleansing blood. Those aprons are starched shields of strength and dignity from the countless burdens and blessings carried within their folds.

See how the apron strings once tied around your waist now pirouette as ribbons of faith declaring God's glory. Our well-worn aprons wave in victory, celebrating the sovereign power, love, grace, and mercy that was unleashed with each syllable of prayer uttered. These precious garments of prayer warriors shine as a rainbow of endless hope.

Let's start an apron movement of prayer! Cinch up your apron strings now. The eternal clothesline awaits!

"Apron Jubilee"
Kay Young Robb

RECIPES

THE ORIGINAL RECIPE FOR PRAYER

READ: MATTHEW 6:5-13

When the disciples asked Jesus to teach them to pray, He gladly obliged and we have this treasure. It is most popularly called the "Lord's Prayer" or the "Disciples' Prayer."

It is likely that you have memorized it or know it very well. When we have memorized something or know it well, we tend to say it by rote, and it often becomes less vibrant and meaningful, even mechanical.

May I urge you to take t-i-m-e with it. Expand it as you pray. I have been doing this for a long time, and it has become richer and more meaningful, as I sense the Holy Spirit revealing to me His heart and His will. I have often read that you learn to pray by praying, and I've found that to be especially true with the Lord's Prayer.

Below is an example of how it can be enlarged and become more comprehensive. It is always evolving. So, for today here is a stream of prayerfulness that may not be grammatically accurate or scripturally perfect. It's just a child of God talking to her Father. My prayer may not even be considered "correct" as I am not a theologian. The important thing is to pray and that God receives the glory. Let the Holy Spirit guide you in your personal expansion. He will.

OUR FATHER, WHO ART IN HEAVEN, HALLOWED BY YOUR NAME

You, our Father, are the One true God alone, worthy of all praise, worship, glory, adoration, exaltation, reverence, and respect. You. Are. Holy. Alone worthy of all praise, thanks, love, and glory. You are on the one true Throne. The only Throne that really matters where all Your splendor, majesty, and glory dwell. You are magnificent, marvelous, beautiful, wonderful, amazing, loving, kind, gracious, and merciful far beyond what all of the saints put together can imagine.

YOUR KINGDOM COME, YOUR WILL BE DONE, ON EARTH AS IT IS IN HEAVEN

Lord, for Your Kingdom that is already here—Your children, I pray for me and my brothers and sisters that we would do Your will. That we would be willing to be willing to "will and do" for Your good pleasure. That we would be obedient, seeking first Your Kingdom and Your righteousness with our priorities in Your order. That we would love You with all our heart, all our mind, all our soul, and all our strength and our neighbors as ourselves. That we would be humble and surrendered servants. That we would be good ambassadors reflecting You.

Lord, I pray that we would not just get glimpses or slices of heaven on earth; but that we would get whole landscapes and whole pies of heaven on earth…for Your glory. That we, and those who don't know You yet, would see Your goodness and greatness in the land of the living. That Your fame would grow. That You would reveal to us who You are and that Your Kingdom would expand—again, for Your glory. It's all about Your glory! That there would be love, unity, harmony, beauty, continual praise and worship of You, light, truth, health, life, safety, and provision. And that is just an inkling, Lord. For I can't even really begin to imagine.

Then, God of the Angel Armies, I ask You to deploy and destroy that which is against Your Kingdom, Your children, Your will, and Your glory. That scorpions would be trampled, snakes crushed, fiery darts extinguished, and every scheme of the enemy thwarted. Send the devil's minions and demons back to hell with "Epic Fail" across their faces. May they be so crushed, crippled, and drowned that they will not be able to return for another assignment. May chaos and confusion reign in the pit where there are no successes. The war is won, Lord! Hallelujah! And I just ask, in our time and space, that battles may be won today. That the scoreboard would read: Satan – 0% and God – 100%. I pray that You would glue shut, with Your victorious blood, the mouth of the roaring lion who seeks to devour us. Don't allow him even one nibble! You are far above any rule, power, dominion, and authority. The King of King and Lord of Lords. The Victor. The Conqueror. The Overcomer, the One who triumphed over sin and death. The Great I Am!

GIVE US THIS DAY OUR DAILY BREAD

Thank You, thank You, thank You, Bread of Life! You have given us everything we need for life and godliness. You supply all our needs according to Your riches in glory, which is everything! You withhold no good thing, and You are the Giver of good gifts. Thank You! Thank You, faithful Father, who takes perfect care of His children; thank You, Good Shepherd, who takes excellent care of His sheep; and thank You, Holy Spirit, who is the ideal companion and ever-present and all-powerful Help in time of trouble. Thank You that You know what we need before we ask. I ask, Lord. I don't know what we need, but You do. You are omnipotent, omnipresent, and omniscient. So I ask, Lord. I ask for provision emotionally, spiritually, mentally, and physically. That we would be able to live the full, complete, and abundant lives You died for us to have. Again, for Your glory, Lord, may it be so.

AND FORGIVE US OUR DEBTS, AS WE FORGIVE OUR DEBTORS

I am sorry, Lord. I do what I don't want to do, and I don't do what I want. May I decrease and You increase. I thank You for Your Fount of Forgiveness that *never* runs dry! Glory, hallelujah to the Lamb that was slain to take away my sins, of which I am the chief. Lord, I thank You that You have removed my sins as far as the east is from the west. Thank You for Your patience, long-suffering, and forbearance with me. Thank You that Your loving sacrifice on the Cross has covered a multitude of sins and there is no condemnation in You. I pray for me and all my brothers and sisters that we would be humble and surrendered and obedient to forgive others. That we would not take the bait of Satan and hold on to offenses. That we would remember the grace and mercy and forgiveness You bestow upon us, be obedient to Your will and Word, and forgive others.

ʻAND LEAD US NOT INTO TEMPTATION, BUT DELIVER US FROM THE EVIL ONE

Oh, Lord, that we would hunger and thirst after You and Your Kingdom and Your righteousness first and foremost. That we would cling to the Vine and not be lukewarm. That the world, the flesh, and the devil would not sway us. That we would keep our eyes on You. That we would not look to the left or right, Lord, and keep our feet from evil, please. That you would yank back Satan's leash, and that whatever he means for evil, You will turn around for good.

A FEW ADDITIONAL TIDBITS FOR WHEN I PRAY THE LORD'S PRAYER:

When saying "Our Father," I love envisioning Jesus and the Holy Spirit joining me as the "Our."

When praying about time and space, be specific with places and dates. I often include tomorrow's date since it could be tomorrow on the other side of the world (depending on what time I pray).

Ask forgiveness for any unconfessed sin. Be specific. I usually have a separate confession time, but sometimes by the time I do that, and the time I am praying this prayer, I've blown it. Keep short accounts of unconfessed sin.

Now, as you read and meditate on Matthew 6:5-13 for yourself, write your impressions here:

Our Recipe for Prayer

Gather your utensils: your time, your heart, your mind, and the Word of God.

May these words of my mouth and this meditation of my heart be pleasing in your sight, LORD, my Rock and my Redeemer (Psalm 19:14).

For the word of God is alive and active. Sharper than any double-edged sword, it penetrates even to dividing soul and spirit, joints and marrow; it judges the thoughts and attitudes of the heart (Hebrews 4:12).

Tie on your aprons, my friends.

"Be dressed ready for service and keep your lamps burning, like men waiting for their master to return from a wedding banquet, so that when he comes and knocks they can immediately open the door for him. It will be good for those servants whose master finds them watching when he comes. I tell you the truth, he will dress himself to serve, will have them recline at the table and come and wait on them. It will be good for those servants whose master finds them ready, even if he comes in the second or third watch of the night. But understand this: If the owner of the house had known at what hour the thief was coming, he would not have let his house be broken into. You must also be ready because the Son of Man will come at an hour when you do not expect Him" (Luke 12:35-40).

Heap an unceasing supply of **Adoration** to God.

My mouth will speak in praise of the Lord. Let every creature praise his holy name forever and ever (Psalm 145:21).

Season liberally with **Praise**.

Great is the Lord, and greatly to be praised. His greatness is unsearchable (Psalm 145:3 NKJV).

Sift out all ingredients that will not result in a sweet aroma by **Repentance**.

If we confess our sins, he is faithful and just and will forgive us our sins and purify us from all unrighteousness (1 John 1:9).

Sprinkle abundantly with **Offerings of thanksgiving**.

Give thanks in all circumstances, for this is God's will for you in Christ Jesus (1 Thessalonians 5:18).

Follow by gently kneading in **Needs and intercessions**.

And my God will meet all your needs according to the riches of his glory in Christ Jesus (Philippians 4:19).

FAMILY RECIPES
FROM MY KITCHEN TO YOURS

Baked Rice Pudding
Virginia Moore (Grandmom)

This was a popular dessert at the diner!

1/2 cup rice

1 quart milk, (4 cups), scalded (Look for tiny bubbles around edge of pan, and remove from heat. Do not let it come to a boil.)

1 cup sugar

1/2 teaspoon salt

1 tablespoon butter

1/8 teaspoon nutmeg or cinnamon (optional)

Combine ingredients and pour into a greased 2-quart glass baking dish.

Bake at 325 degrees for approximately 2 hours or until rice is tender.

Stir occasionally, folding in the brown layer that will form on top.

Cool and refrigerate unless serving that day.

Grandmom's Applesauce
Virginia Moore (Grandmom)

Kids of all ages love this!

A mix of apples (some tart) to yield 14 cups	2 cups water
	1 cup sugar (or to taste)

Wash, core, and seed apples (do not pare) and cut into chunks to equal 14 cups.

Combine apples and water in large, covered pot and bring to a boil. Simmer on low heat until apples are very soft. Stir occasionally to avoid scorching.

Pour apples into a sieve over a big bowl, saving the apple water.

Strain, using a food mill to remove the peels.

Return apple content and liquid in bowl to the pot.

Stir in ½ cup sugar and increase, as needed, to taste.

Cook about five minutes more, and add water as needed for your preferred consistency.

Yield: 8 cups

This freezes well. Leave enough space in containers for expansion.

Mother Moore's Chicken Pot Pie
Virginia Moore (Grandmom)

Everyone loved the days when Chicken Pot Pie was on the menu at the diner—a perennial favorite! (This is close to what Southerners refer to as Chicken and Dumplings.)

1 small chicken, cut into parts
1 teaspoon salt
1 medium onion, chopped
4 medium potatoes, cut into quarters or eighths
½ cup celery, chopped
Carrots, sliced, may also be added for color and flavor, if desired
2 tablespoons chopped parsley
Pepper, to taste

Cover chicken with water (about 2 quarts), and add salt and onion.

Simmer until tender (about 35 minutes).

Remove chicken, and when cool enough, take the meat off the bones.

Bring the unstrained chicken broth to a boil.

Add celery and potatoes.

Gradually add dough squares (recipe follows) into the boiling broth, stirring often to prevent sticking.

Add parsley and chicken (in bite-size pieces) and simmer about

30 minutes, until dough squares are cooked.

Season with pepper, to taste.

Dough Squares

2 cups flour

½ teaspoon salt

3 eggs

2-3 tablespoons water

Combine flour and salt in mixing bowl.

Beat water and eggs with fork.

Slowly add to flour mixture stirring with fork until it forms a soft but not sticky dough.

Place dough on floured surface.

Knead about two minutes.

Divide dough in half.

Roll to about 1/8" thick.

Cut into two-inch squares.

Shoofly Pie
Grammy Yocum (Great-Grandmom)

This recipe came from my great-grandmother who died before I was born. While I didn't know her, I treasure a handwritten note that she inscribed to her daughter in a devotional book, *God's Minute* (that belonged to my grandmother, my mom, and is now mine). The inscription reads:

> *Virginia,*
> *The all wise, all loving, all adjusting power of Christ is now lifted up in me, filling me with enduring health and strength. I trust in God and am not afraid.*
>
> *Mother*

As her great-granddaughter, I don't know the circumstances surrounding the note, but the truth of it prevails to all generations. Hallelujah!

Liquid Bottom

To ½ cup boiling water, stir in ½ teaspoon baking soda. Then add ½ cup dark Karo syrup* until mixed well. Set aside to cool.

*Molasses can be substituted, if preferred.

Crumbs

1 cup flour

½ cup brown sugar

Pinch salt

1 teaspoon cinnamon

Blend together well with fingers to make crumbs.

Add 2 tablespoons Crisco or butter; cut into mixture.

Pour cooled liquid into unbaked 8-inch pie crust.

Sprinkle ¾ of the crumbs on top, adding the last ¼ after 15 minutes of baking.

Bake at 350 degrees for 30 minutes.

Mom's Sand Tarts
Sally Reeser (Mom)

These were our traditional Christmas cookies. Nothing says Christmas like a Sand Tart.

1 pound butter
2 cups sugar
3 eggs, beaten
1 teaspoon vanilla

4 cups flour
1 tablespoon baking powder
½ teaspoon salt

Cream softened butter and sugar until fluffy.

Add eggs and vanilla.

Mix thoroughly.

Mix flour, baking powder, and salt.

Add to wet mixture a little at a time until thoroughly mixed.

Place heaping teaspoon on cookie sheet in a round shape or roll out dough and use a festive cookie cutter.

Optional: Add a pecan half OR cinnamon sugar mixture (traditional Pennsylvania Dutch) on top before baking, or any desired sprinkle for decoration.

Bake at 375 degrees 8 to 10 minutes or until slightly brown.

Place on rack to cool.

Baked Cup Custards

Another favorite at the diner. They sold out fast!

4 eggs	½ teaspoon vanilla
½ cup sugar	4 cups milk
½ teaspoon salt	Nutmeg (optional)

Beat eggs slightly.

Add sugar, salt, and vanilla.

Scald milk and pour it slowly over egg mixture.

Stir until thoroughly mixed.

Pour into custard cups, filling them two-thirds full.

Sprinkle with nutmeg if desired.

Set cups in a pan and pour hot water around them until it comes to the level of the custard.

Bake at 325 degrees approximately 40 minutes, or until a silver knife comes out clean when inserted in the center of the custard. The baking time could take up to an hour.

To unmold custards, they must be thoroughly chilled. Custard may also be baked in a casserole. Serve with whipped cream if desired.

Makes 8 custards.

Mabel Yoder, Grantsville, MD; Mrs. I. B. Lapp, Oley, PA

© Mennonite Community Cookbook, Herald Press. Used with permission. All rights reserved.

White Bear Inn Dip
Kathy May (Sister)

Great holiday and party dip!

2 – 8 oz. Philadelphia Cream Cheese blocks (at room temperature)
1 packet of George Washington Golden Seasoning (found with bouillon in store or online)
Black, chopped olives, half of a 4.25 oz. can (or to taste), drained
1 teaspoon horseradish
Dash of garlic salt

Mix cream cheese with mixer until fluffy.

Add all other ingredients.

Mix until well blended.

Store in refrigerator; bring to room temperature before serving.

Serve with crackers.

White Bear Inn was located on a bucolic, wooded road outside of the town of Birdsboro, Pennsylvania, where I grew up. Opened in 1810, the inn was a "station" on the Underground Railroad for fleeing slaves seeking refuge. White Bear Inn's restaurant was a popular dining spot over the years and a family favorite for special occasions, such as my parents' 25th wedding anniversary. The dip was a specialty item that locals loved; many former customers continue the nostalgic tradition in their homes after the inn closed, due to repeated flooding from the nearby Hay Creek.

Pennsylvania Dutch Potato Filling
Virginia Moore (Grandmom)

Most of the country makes their filling, or stuffing, using strictly bread. The Pennsylvania Dutch are known for their filling using potatoes. Another diner favorite!

- 5-6 medium potatoes, peeled and cut into bite-size chunks
- ½ cup milk
- ½ teaspoon salt
- ¼ teaspoon pepper
- One stick of butter (8 tablespoons), divided
- 1 cup onion, diced
- 3 stalks celery, diced
- 4-5 cups cubed, stale bread or cubed stuffing mix
- 2 eggs, lightly beaten
- ¼ cup fresh parsley, chopped

Preheat oven to 350 degrees.

Generously butter (approx. 2 tablespoons) a 2-quart baking dish.

Cook potatoes until soft, and then drain, mash, and beat in milk.

Add salt and pepper to taste.

Melt 4 tablespoons butter in large skillet over medium heat.

Add onions and celery; cook until soft.

With slotted spoon, combine with potatoes.

Sauté bread cubes in same skillet until crispy.

Add to potatoes, along with the eggs and parsley.

Mix well and place into buttered casserole.

Dot with 2 tablespoons of butter.

Bake 35-40 minutes until brown on top.

Aggie's Chocolate Pound Cake
Aggie Collier (Grandmother-in-law)

This is my husband's grandmother's recipe. I did not have the privilege of knowing her, but I love seeing photos of her. She was always "dressed to the nines" with impeccable hair, makeup, and nails. This recipe, a crown jewel in her recipe box, was included in her church's cookbook put together by the members of the Ladies Aid group. However, the recipe was printed without the key ingredient: ½ cup of cocoa. No one noticed the omission until someone tried the recipe. Was the omission because she did not want to reveal her prized recipe? A mystery that will never be solved this side of heaven!

½ pound butter
3 cups sugar
½ cup Crisco
3 cups flour

½ cup cocoa
5 eggs
¼ teaspoon vanilla
1¼ cups milk

Cream butter, sugar, and Crisco.

Sift flour and add to the other ingredients.

Grease and flour tube pan.

Bake for 1 hour and 25 minutes at 300 degrees.

Icing

2 cups sugar
1 stick of butter
1/4 cup cocoa

1/4 teaspoon salt
2/3 cup milk

Mix ingredients and bring to a boil for 2 minutes, stirring constantly.

Remove from heat and add 1 teaspoon vanilla. Beat until creamy.

Hot Chicken Salad Casserole
Luc Albee (Friend)
Luc is also Ida Scudder's niece!

4 cups chicken, cooked
3 hard-boiled eggs, chopped
1 cup celery, chopped
½ cup green pepper, chopped
½ cup mayonnaise
1 cup slivered almonds, toasted
2 tablespoons pimiento, chopped
2 tablespoons lemon juice
1 can cream of chicken soup

Mix all ingredients together and pour into large casserole. Top with the following mixture:

> Up to 1 cup Kraft Velveeta or cheddar cheese, grated
> 3 cups of potato chips, crushed = about 1½ cups

Bake at 350 degrees for 25 minutes. Serves 6.

Spinach Salad
Luc Albee (Friend)

Dressing
(Make at least 6 hours ahead.)

1 cup oil (not olive oil)
5 tablespoons red wine vinegar
4 tablespoons sour cream
1½ teaspoons salt
½ teaspoon dry mustard
1 teaspoon sugar
2 teaspoons chopped parsley
2 cloves garlic, or to taste, minced or mashed
Coarsely ground pepper

Salad

1-2 bunches fresh spinach or 8 oz. bag
4 hard-boiled eggs, chopped
6-8 bacon strips, fried and crumbled (or equivalent of bottled bacon bits)
1/4 pound fresh mushrooms, sliced
3 green onions, chopped (using the white part only)
1/3 cup Parmesan cheese, grated

Add dressing and serve immediately.

Thank-Mas Pie
Becky Terry

I make this only around the holidays of Thanksgiving and Christmas; thus, the name. This recipe was given to me by Rhonda, a friend I worked with at Coca-Cola USA. The original name of the recipe was Japanese Fruit Pie. That name didn't ever seem to fit, so I changed it. This is so easy and so good. I make it for my sister-in-law and brother-in-law every year—they love it!

- 1½ sticks of margarine or butter, melted (not hot)
- 2 cups sugar
- 4 eggs
- 1 tablespoon vinegar
- 1 cup raisins, black or golden (boiled for a minute to make them plump, then drain)
- 1 cup coconut (flaked or shredded)
- 1 cup pecans, chopped
- Chocolate chips, add to suit (optional)
- 2 frozen pie shells

Combine first four ingredients and mix well.

Add remaining ingredients and mix well.

Pour into pie shells.

Bake at 300 degrees for 50 minutes. Can check with toothpick for doneness.

Onion-Crusted Chicken
Becky Terry

I tore this recipe out of a newspaper as a newlywed, and it is my family's favorite.

- 2 pounds boneless chicken breasts
- 1 stick butter or margarine
- 1 tablespoon dry mustard
- 1 tablespoon Worcestershire sauce
- Few drops Tabasco sauce (optional)
- 1 container (6 oz.) of French's Original Crispy Fried Onions

Melt butter.

Add the next three ingredients and mix well.

Crush fried onions (I just put them into a baggie and smash).

Dip chicken into butter mixture and then onion rings, coating well.

Note: The extra butter can be poured into the bottom of the pan, and the onions on top will remain crispy. Or pour the butter over the top for moist fried onions.

Bake at 350 degrees for 30 minutes.

MORE DINER MORSELS

Our popular diner closed only on Christmas and New Year's Eve. Our family would gather there Christmas Day for a private celebration. We didn't have to worry about enough oven space, and we just stacked up the dirty dishes for the dishwasher the next morning. The phone would ring continually to see if we were open for business, and many cars would drive into the parking lot looking for a place to eat. I felt bad for them, but extremely grateful for the one day of respite for our family. It gave us a chance to be together, celebrate Christmas, and enjoy our time work-free.

Most of my relatives worked at the diner at one time or another. Aunt Kay managed it, my cousin, Debbie, was second-in-command, Uncle Edward ran the business side, Uncle Bill was the maintenance man, my mom and grandmom were the cooks, and then the rest of us worked as waitresses, or wherever we were needed on any given day. And that was just our side of the family; my aunt's side of the family were vital employees as well. Like any family-run business, it was a huge part of our lives.

Since Grandmom never learned to drive, she conveniently lived next-door to the diner, just a parking lot away. She started her shift in the early evening and stayed until the wee hours of the morning. After her retirement, we teased her for being nocturnal, since her sleeping schedule never returned to normal hours. At all hours of the night, she'd still be clipping recipes from magazines with pinking shears and gluing them to old Christmas cards. That practice lasted way into her 90s; she lived to be 104.

One Sunday afternoon while working at the diner as a young teenager, I was "taking cash." An older, distinguished gentleman approached me at the cashier's station and asked me if he could give me some advice on my makeup. I wondered what could possibly be wrong with my beautiful blue eyeshadow that covered my entire eyelid. But, intrigued, I said, "Sure." He told me he was Debbie Reynold's makeup artist and in town with her while she performed at the Valley Forge Music Fair. He gave me some helpful makeup tips, telling me to use a light ivory base on the whole eyelid and a brown shade in the crease as a contour. I made my mom stop at the drugstore on the way home that evening to get the items he recommended, and I still use them to this day.

The Limerick Diner is now under new ownership. The Moore's Colonial Limerick Diner, as it was officially called and known, is no longer in existence after five decades. The end of an era, but memories remain. The people are forever etched in my heart. Uncle Edward, the owner, passed away in 2019 at the age of 91. I had the privilege and honor to speak at his memorial service. He nicknamed me "Becky Graham" as I often spoke to him about my faith in Jesus Christ. My last conversation with him was about Billy Graham's funeral. Uncle Edward was very animated as he told me he watched every minute.

He relayed to me, "You know, Billy's son said that sin is a soul disease." He paused for a moment and then said, "Well, there is no antibiotic for that."

Well actually, Uncle Edward, there is! His name is Jesus! He bore all your sin-disease on the Cross to completely heal us spiritually.

Dear reader, if for any reason you have done this Bible study but have not asked Jesus to be your Savior, NOW is the perfect time! A simple prayer is all that is needed:

"God, I believe Jesus Christ is Your Son who came to earth to die for my sins. I am sorry for my sins, and I ask for forgiveness as I place my trust in Jesus as my Savior. Thank You for making me a new creation in You and for the gift of eternal life!"

My friend, heaven awaits! Wonder if there will be a diner? The Divine Diner, perhaps, serving lots of divinity and angel food cake. I'll be there, and I look forward to seeing you there too!

The Old Diner

Uncle Edward and Aunt Kay bought the original diner in 1956, which we lovingly referred to as the "old diner." Here's the backstory to their purchase: As the owner of the gas station next door to the diner, my uncle ate his meals there but described the food as "terrible." When the diner went up for sale, Uncle Edward believed he could improve the business, especially with his wife's experience as a waitress at another diner. Aunt Kay initially resisted, but with the support of extended family on both sides, the venture led to success. I still remember the wonder as a young child of entering the curious world of the diner through the back door. I marveled at the exotic equipment of the steam table, the huge grill, and the commercial dishwasher. However, I learned to stay out of the way of the constant hustle-bustle until I was old enough to work there, starting with peeling potatoes.

The New Diner

The diner became so popular and successful that my aunt and uncle bought a parcel of land across the street for what became the "new diner," completed in 1970. The "old diner" was eventually torn down.

Vintage Postcard

This postcard depicts the "new diner." Fun facts: My dad is seated at the counter (fourth one down with the blue pants, and his Buick is the first one on the left in the parking lot.) As one of the few family members who didn't work at the diner, he just happened to be there for the photo—a total fluke. My grandmother lived in the white house beyond the sign, which was convenient since she never learned to drive. Can you imagine that dear little lady crossing that parking lot in the wee hours of the morning? One more tidbit: I occasionally see this postcard pop up on eBay for a hefty price!

Grandmom's Birthday

My grandmother taking a break from cooking at the old diner to celebrate her birthday. The beautiful mural behind her spanned two walls and depicted Pennsylvania Dutch life.

Grandmom and Gertrude

Grandmom, our night cook, shown here in her 80s with Gertrude, our longtime day cook, who stopped by on her day off to catch a hug from "Mother Moore." From the pearled barley on the counter and perhaps onions in her hand, I imagine my grandmom was in the middle of making soup.

A Familiar Sight and Smile

My mom cooking away! One time a young cook spilled a huge pot of boiling water on my mom's leg, requiring a skin graft and an extended stay in the hospital. Of course, Mom returned to work, and the other cook, while appalled by the accident, also remained employed there a long time.

A Day on the Job

Here I am "taking cash" at the register. In the history of the diner, only cash was accepted for payment. My uncle insisted that all the bills face the same way in the drawer. Behind me are Lance crackers, one of the "impulse items" we sold, along with candy bars and cigars from the case under the register. (The emptied cigar boxes became favorites of family members for storage.) York peppermint patties sat on the counter and sold for two cents each.

Our Own Version of Laverne and Shirley

My pal, Nancy, and I, wearing our traditional uniforms and taking a break in the back parking lot. (We wore red aprons during the Christmas season.) Uncle Bill, my grandmom's brother, is standing on the back porch. He could fix anything and worked as our handyman for many years. My aunt's Buick Riviera is behind us.

A Rare Respite

Nancy and I taking a late morning break during our shift, 6 a.m.-2 p.m. Construction workers came up from Philadelphia to work on a nuclear power plant and stopped at our diner for an early breakfast. After that crush of business, a steady stream of breakfast customers kept us busy until a little lull before an equally busy lunch. Note the jukeboxes at each table.

A Merry Christmas

My husband, Jim, and my mom, Sally, on Christmas Day in the dining room. Christmas was the only day of the year we closed the diner for our family celebration.

Christmas Day Feast

After I married and moved from Pennsylvania to Georgia, Jim and I—and later our twin girls—would fly home every Christmas, never wanting to miss that special occasion. We enjoyed the roominess of the diner and the rare event of everyone having the same day off. Lots of food, gifts, and love!

Acknowledgments

The "Pantry Provisions" lists originated with Sylvia Gunter and are used here with her permission. They can be found in her book, *Prayer Portions*. She also has written two volumes titled *Prayer Essentials for Living in His Presence*. I highly recommend all her materials. You can find them at Amazon as well as her website: @thefathersbusiness.com. My heartfelt thanks to Sylvia for her wonderful example to me as both a woman after God's own heart and a prayer warrior.

My deep gratitude to Judy Gordon Morrow for her guidance and encouragement. Her expertise "beefed up" this Bible study. My appreciation to LeAnne Martin whose support brought me to the "finish line."

And, to the only worthy One who has given His all so that I would have all, my Lord and Savior, Jesus Christ. Thank You, my God and my King, for paying the ultimate penalty and price to give me everything I need for life and godliness.

Thank You for the amazing gift of prayer and for the privilege and honor of being able to talk to You anytime, anywhere, anyhow. Thank You that You hear me, listen to me, care about what I say, interpret perfectly, intercede faithfully, and answer sovereignly according to Your infinite wisdom, power, and love. To You be all glory and praise, thanks and love.

I love the Lord, for he heard my voice;
He heard my cry for mercy.
Because he turned his ear to me, I will
call on him as long as I live.
Psalm 116:1-2

Soli Deo Gloria—Glory to God alone!

Connect with Becky!
She'd love to hear from you.

beckyreeserterry@gmail.com

Recommended Inspirational Reading

The Practice of God's Presence by Andrew Murray

The Power of Prayer in a Believer's Life by Charles Spurgeon

Ida Scudder: Healing Bodies, Touching Hearts by Janet Benge

Susanna Wesley by Charles Ludwig

Evidence Not Seen: A Woman's Miraculous Faith in the Jungles of World War II by Darlene Deibler Rose

The Audacious Molly Bruno: Amazing Stories from the Life of a Powerful Woman of Prayer by Marie Armenia

Operation World: The Definitive Prayer Guide to Every Nation by Jason Mandryk

www.ingramcontent.com/pod-product-compliance
Lightning Source LLC
Chambersburg PA
CBHW051431290426
44109CB00016B/1508